The Boy and the Jaguar

by

Terri Daneshyar

First published in 2023

www.terridaneshyar.com

Cover design by Leo Hartas

Illustrations by Alan Sharpe

ISBN-10: 9798394769870

Contents

Prologue   1

Chapter One – A New Discovery   3

Chapter Two - Pok-a-tok   12

Chapter Three - Lost   24

Chapter Four - First Meeting   34

Chapter Five - Jealousy   49

Chapter Six - Snakeskin   58

Chapter Seven - The King's Hunter   73

Chapter Eight - Rescue   85

Chapter Nine - A Close Encounter   95

Chapter Ten - Revelations   105

Chapter Eleven - The King's Offering   112

Chapter Twelve - Celebrations   120

Chapter Thirteen - Visitors and Gossip   133

Chapter Fourteen - Desolation   139

Chapter Fifteen - An Unexpected Outcome   148

Part Two

Chapter Sixteen - Ixchel is Gone   159

Chapter Seventeen - Snakebite   166

Chapter Eighteen - Conscripts   174

Chapter Nineteen - Training   180

Chapter Twenty - Bad Omen   188

Chapter Twenty-One - Eloy's Appeal   196

Chapter Twenty-Two - A Trap is Set   202

Chapter Twenty-Three - Reunited   212

Chapter Twenty-Four - The Black Jaguar   218

Chapter Twenty-Five - Farewell   227

Epilogue   236

Author's Note   238

Acknowledgements   239

About the Author   241

Works published by Terri Daneshyar   242

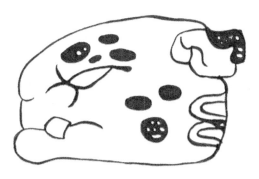

Mayan Symbol for Jaguar

The Prophecy:

He who walks with jaguars shall know true greatness.

Prologue

Deep within the tropical rainforest in the time of the ancient Mayans, Ek Balem, Jaguar Lord of the Underworld, patrolled, listening, waiting. The quiet of the night was broken by the moans of a woman in childbirth. The moon approached the zenith when the month would change from Zip to Zotz. Balem paced anxiously. He must arrive soon if he is to have the deep wisdom associated with this month. The moans ceased and the unmistakeable sound of a baby's first cry reached

1

his ears. Good, he thought, the boy is on time, now the prophecy may come to fruition. He continued on his way; the bright moonlight holding no fear for him, his black coat the perfect camouflage. No-one would see him.

In the hour after midnight as the night edged towards morning, the woman's moans began again but this time there was no welcoming cry, only silence, then sobbing. Balem, curiosity aroused, returned to the settlement and watched as a woman lay a small bundle on the ground behind the wooden hut that housed the other baby. She returned to the new mother. The jaguar approached the bundle. Inside lay a tiny baby, still and silent. *A second child, born in Zotz, a night creature. This is unexpected,* he thought. He leaned in, licked its face and breathed life into it. The infant opened its eyes and reached out to touch the big cat's whiskers. Balem held the child in his gaze and blessed it. 'Cry out little one,' he said, 'they will come.' And then he vanished into the undergrowth.

The baby, weak as it was, cried quietly until the midwife came out to investigate. Picking up the child, she ran back inside.

'You have been blessed Abha, your daughter lives. Balem be praised.'

Chapter One

A New Discovery

Perched high in a tree, overlooking the pathways, sat a small girl. Her stillness and balance matched that of a cat as she waited for the hunters. Here, amongst the dense rainforest foliage, she felt at home. She could find her way easily and moved so quietly that the animals rarely noticed her. She climbed the trees with the ease of a feline and would sit for hours in the branches studying the knots and whorls in the wood, or the veins of the leaves, or the insects that ran up and down intent on their purpose. The trees accepted her calm presence and never once let her fall even if she climbed to their highest branches. From this vantage point she could see the vast expanse of rainforest in one direction and the rising pyramid at the heart of the city in the other. For now, though, she was focused on her pursuers. *I hear you,* she thought listening to the sound of leaves being brushed to one side. Below her, a tall boy held up an arm to halt his group.

'She is near,' he whispered, 'be vigilant.' His pack of followers looked about, adrenalin pumping. Would they catch her today?

Ixchel, stretched languidly and crept through the branches from tree to tree, always watching her hunters. Even though they scoured the tree tops they could not see her. Rustling in the undergrowth produced a yell from a boy at the rear of the group. In a panic he threw out his net but all he caught was a porcupine, its sharp spines getting tangled, immobilising it. The frightened animal squealed and grunted but the boy, embarrassed by his mistake, ignored it and ran to catch up with the others who had moved on, aware that his shout would have alerted their prey.

Checking carefully that there were no stragglers from the hunting party still lurking, Ixchel, climbed down from the tree and went to help the porcupine which had so exhausted itself trying to get free that it lay still. Ixchel bent down, frightened eyes investigated hers.

'Well, you are in a mess little one. Let me see what I can do.'

Very gently, she lifted the bundle and retreated to the undergrowth so that they would both be hidden from view.

'We don't want those boys to find us,' she whispered. Laying the creature on the ground, Ixchel reached for her small flint blade that she often carried. The animal waited patiently as deft fingers began cutting and untangling the net fibres from its spines. It was a painful process; several times she cut her fingers on the sharp spikes. Eventually, her efforts were rewarded, and the porcupine was free. Instead of running off, it offered thanks and then shed a spine. 'Take this sister,' it said. 'My name is Silas. When you are in need, plant this in the ground and help will come.' Then it shuffled off into the rainforest.

'Wait!'

She followed after it, but it had disappeared into the greenery. Puzzled, she retraced her steps and picked up the spine, it was quite beautiful, covered in a striated pattern of black, brown and white. *Did*

I really understand that creature? Surely not and yet… She pushed the spine through her black hair, *no-one will notice it there.*

While she was wondering how she had perfectly understood when the porcupine spoke to her, a scent of boy reached her nostrils. Springing catlike, she was up the nearest tree, peering down as the hunters returned.

Whooping with delight, she pounced, landing on the back of the boy in charge.

'I win again, Eloy,' she yelled delightedly. 'You are too noisy to catch me.'

Despite his disappointment, Eloy burst out laughing.

'One day little sister I will catch you. One day.'

The other boys gathered around. 'How did you avoid us?'

'How come we never see you?'

'How do you climb the trees so easily?'

So many questions. Ixchel merely shrugged them off and headed back to the settlement arm-in-arm with her twin brother.

'Eloy, I must tell you what happened today. After that idiot boy caught a porcupine, I climbed down to free it.'

'As only you would,' grinned Eloy.

'Yes, yes, but then it spoke to me. I mean it really spoke.'

Eloy stopped. 'How?'

'I don't know, but I understood it. Truly.'

'What did it say then? Thanks for the rescue.'

'Yes, but it then it gave me this,' she said, pulling the spine from her hair, 'And it said if ever I need help, plant this in the ground and help will come.'

Eloy knew she wouldn't lie and yet it was hard to believe. The rest of the hunting party had dispersed so he grabbed her hand, pulling her back into the forest, startling an iguana that was basking under a tree.

The lizard looked at the children and scuttled off.

'Did it say anything?' asked Eloy.

'Nothing,' said Ixchel.

'Wait here.' He ran into the trees and returned carrying another smaller iguana which thrashed about in his hands. Endeavouring to hold it still, he held it out to Ixchel.

'Talk to it.'

'And say what?'

'I don't know. Ask it its name.'

Ixchel reached out to lay a hand on the animal's head. It immediately became still.

'Be calm my friend. We won't harm you.'

'Anything?' asked Eloy, then before she could reply the lizard nipped his finger.

'Ow!' he yelled, dropping his captive, which dashed away before either of them could react.'

'Did it speak to you?'

'No,' said Ixchel, disappointedly. Eloy too, looked a little crestfallen.

'You do believe me, don't you?' said Ixchel.

'Maybe,' he shrugged, but really, he knew she had been truthful. 'Let's go home.'

Their mother was waiting for them when they got back.

'Where have you been? Your father needs your help in the fields, Eloy. The men have been working since daybreak. Take this food with you and a water pouch,' she said, handing him a large chunk of maize bread. 'Go. Now.'

He ran off quickly, Ixchel was about to follow when she felt a firm grasp on her arm.

'You are coming with me to make the next lot of bread.'

'But I hate cooking,' moaned Ixchel.

'Hate it or not, it is your place. You are nearly nine and you must be schooled in these things if you are to make a good wife one day.'

Ixchel gave her mother a hard stare.

'And don't pout. It will make you ugly. Your brother is handsome but you, I fear, with your rounded head will be hard to marry off.'

Far from being disheartened by her forehead being a different shape to the other children, Ixchel loved the fact she was different. It wasn't just her face. Her body was lithe and nimble, not stocky as the other girls. She could squeeze into small places and was never more at home than when she was in her beloved rainforest. Apart from her brother, who was tall and fearless, the other children were wary of the rainforest, scared of the creatures who lurked there. They only ventured in when they had to or when Eloy pressed them into playing the hunting game. These children would grow up to be farmers and hunters of small mammals, but Eloy had his sights set on

9

becoming a warrior. Although how the son of a farmer could achieve this he did not know. He made spears and practised throwing them long distances. He threw a knife with ease, and skilfully gutted fish or skinned the agouti, caught for food. The blow pipes he loved, often shooting the hard clay pellets at any of the children who teased his little sister. He could also use them to accurately knock large insects from the branches, often picking out ones the others couldn't see with his sharp eyesight and good aim. Soon he would learn to use a bow and arrow and then he would be the ultimate hunter.

Their parents worried about both children.

'The boy is too headstrong. How will I ever make a farmer of him?' said their father.

'Ixchel refuses to learn to cook,' said their mother. 'How will she ever marry?'

Despite their worries, they loved their children deeply, especially Ixchel, who had only just survived at birth, and indeed for the first year of her life her parents were relieved to wake up each day and find her alive because she was so weak. So convinced were they that she wouldn't survive, they hadn't followed the usual custom of attaching boards to her head as a newborn, to flatten her forehead, or taken her to the community leader for a naming ceremony until she passed her first birthday. He had consulted the calendar before settling on the name Ixchel, after the jaguar goddess of midwifery, due to the unusual circumstances surrounding her birth. Since then, she had flourished even though she remained much smaller than her twin, whose growth far outstripped any of the other children in the village. He was taller, faster, stronger, than any child the community had ever seen. Only Ixchel could match him for speed.

'One day, brother, I will outrun you,' she said later that evening, as they raced around the village, chased by the other children.

'Never,' smiled Eloy. But in his heart, he feared that she might.

Chapter Two

Pok-a-tok

One evening, shortly after the twins' ninth birthday, their father returned from the maize fields in great excitement.

'King Cadmael's warriors have returned from their battle. Tomorrow there is to be a pok-a-tok game against the prisoners.'

'Pok-a-tok,' said Eloy. 'Please can we go and watch it. I have never seen an actual game.'

'We will all go.' said Hadwin. 'Your mother can buy supplies while we are there. The king has promised food and drink if we win and special honours for the players. It will be a great day.'

They talked incessantly over supper about what they would see and do the next day. Only Ixchel was quiet. The city frightened her with its stone walls, high buildings and crowds of strangers.

'Father, I don't want to go,' she said.

'Nonsense child, we are all going. Your mother will need your help.'

'But I don't like the city. I prefer the rainforest.'

'You spend too much time in that forest and not enough helping your mother.'

Ixchel opened her mouth to respond, but her father's raised hand told her to stop.

'You are coming with us and that is an end to it.'

After giving her father a defiant stare, she folded her arms and sat with her head down.

Eloy squeezed her arm gently, then to lighten the mood he asked to hear the story of the hero twins.

'Please father, please.'

Hadwin smiled at his son, 'Get yourselves into bed and I will tell the tale.'

Eloy pulled Ixchel, still sulking, over to their sleeping corner.

'Why is he making me go tomorrow?' she whispered. 'It's not fair.'

'Because a visit to the city is an event and he wants us all to be part of it,' said Eloy. 'He thinks we will enjoy it. Surely you can see that.'

'I suppose,' said Ixchel, grudgingly, snuggling up next to Eloy under their blanket.

When the children were settled, Hadwin sat cross-legged beside them and began the story of the wonderful twins:

'In the ancient days, there were two brothers, wizard kings, sons of the maize god, whose skill at pok-a-tok was greater than any man on earth. As you know, this game is played with a rubber ball on a stone court in which the players score points by getting the ball in their opponent's area and is won by getting the ball through one of the stone rings high up on the wall of the court. The real skill though, is that players cannot use their hands only their knees, hips, elbows and wrists.'

The twins' eyes grew wide as they listened again to the rules of the game.

'That is so difficult,' said Ixchel.

'You say that every time we hear this tale,' laughed Eloy.

'Their skill was so great,' continued Hadwin, 'that their enemies, the wizard kings of Xibalba, the Dark Land, grew jealous and asked them to come and play. While they were there, one of the brothers met and married the princess of Xibalba. The brothers proved themselves unbeatable at the game so in their jealousy the wicked kings of the Dark Land, killed them.'

'I don't like that part,' said Eloy.

'But wait,' said Hadwin. 'The princess escaped Xibalba with her twin babies.'

'Twins like us,' said Ixchel.

'Yes,' said Hadwin. 'Except these were twin boys. The princess took them to their father's mother and asked her to raise them. Shortly after this, the princess died.'

'That's so sad,' said Ixchel, 'I wish she didn't. I would miss our mother if she died.' She looked over at Abha who was busy preparing food for the next day.

'Me too,' said Eloy.

Hadwin smiled at his children, 'Shall I get back to the story?'

'Yes please,' they both said together, holding hands under their blanket.

'The twins grew fast, but they were boisterous and noisy and annoyed their grandmother, so she sent them into the rainforest for a while to fend for themselves; and they were so clever and cunning they always found food. Eventually the queen relented and had them back to live with her. In the palace they turned to magic; after all, they said, our father was a wizard king and our mother was the daughter of the Demon King which means that we have magical powers. So, the boys became skilful at magic, learning spells and charms for strength and protection, but this didn't burn up their energy. They were still very boisterous, and the old queen was tired. To wear them out she had them taught to play pok-a-tok. They became experts at the game and their fame spread. This annoyed the Dark Lords of Xibalba. As a punishment, they summoned the twins to their court. The queen begged them not to go, scared of the same fate that met their father but they said, 'fear not we shall triumph'.

In Xibalba, as well as pok-a-tok, which they won every time, the twins were set many challenges; crossing a river of blood; being offered a seat of honour that because of their magic they knew was red hot; so they refused. They were sent to sleep in the House of Lances, where spears were hurled at them throughout the night; the House of Fire whose red-hot flames tried to consume them; and the House of the Jaguars but instead of attacking, the cats remained docile, by their magic the twins were able to survive every challenge.

You cannot harm us said the twins to the Dark Lords, for we each hold a charm. To prove it, slay us one by one and we will come to life again, so long as we hold the charms. Then the Dark Lords struck first one twin then the other and they rose again, whole, unwounded, and younger and stronger than before.'

'Hooray,' came a pair of very sleepy voices.

'Then the Dark Lords begged for the charms for themselves, and the twins handed over small pieces of jade carved into the shape of a twisted serpent. As soon as they had them, the Dark Lords bade their most faithful servants to strike them dead so that they too might rise up younger and stronger than before. The servants did as they were asked but the Dark Lords remained dead for the charms meant nothing; it was the twins special magic that had saved them. They escaped Xibalba and went back to their grandmother who was overjoyed at their return.'

By the time he had finished, the twins were curled up asleep. Eloy lay with a protective arm around his sister. *Always the strong one,* thought

Hadwin. 'Sleep well children,' he whispered, before slipping away to his own bed.

They were up at dawn, joining the other villagers heading for the city walls, the maize crops left unattended for once. Ixchel listened to the excited voices with a growing sense of dread, fearful of the crowds they would encounter.

The city was protected by a double wall. To enter they had to pass through the first opening and then walk along a narrow passageway between the two walls until they reached the second opening that led into the area in front of the main gate. Already this space was filled with visitors, jostling for position, eager to get a good spot for watching the game. The main entrance was up a series of stone steps designed so that as you climbed, your head was bowed in respect to the gods. Being in such close proximity to so many people was agonising for Ixchel; how she longed for the comfort of a tree. Eventually, it was their turn to climb the steps and enter the heaving heart of the city.

Eloy was enchanted. From left to right he saw people dressed in brightly coloured costumes. It was like being surrounded by rainbows. The headdresses were as attractive as jewels, with their turquoise and red. Many were crowned with

18

feathers. Several times he reached out to touch one as they passed him. Ixchel pressed close to her mother; Eloy, in contrast, gazed excitedly around him, breathing in the atmosphere and the noise. A great cacophony of voices filled the air, people shouting to friends or vendors calling out their wares. All were being pulled along in the direction of the enormous pok-a-tok court in the centre of the city. The large rectangular area had two long sloping walls with stone doughnut shaped rings high up on each of them. The walls were topped with wide steps where the noble families sat to watch the game. Above them was the seating for the priests. The king would be watching proceedings from his throne near the top of an imposing pyramid that faced the end of the court.

Hadwin tried to find a good vantage point for his family to watch the game but as the farmers and poorer people had to stand on the flat ground it was difficult to get a decent view. Most of the noble families were in their seats when the high priests arrived adorned in long cloaks and wearing the most elaborate headdresses. Each wide band was decorated with jade, feathers and shells. The more important the priest, the bigger the headdress.

Once the priests were settled the crowd hushed, awaiting the arrival of King Cadmael. He did not disappoint, striding out of his palace dressed in jaguar skins to show his courage and godlike status. His headdress towered above many of the others, with its elaborate carving of a wooden mask topped with the sun and moon wrapped by a serpent and finished with some metre long feathers and the highly prized turquoise and red feathers of the quetzal bird.

Ixchel's head ached at the sight of the jaguar skins and her chest hurt as if she could feel the spears that had killed each animal. She turned away, retching. Slipping free of her mother's hand she pushed her way back through the crowd, edging outwards and down pathways leading away from the centre. Here it was much less crowded, and her racing heart gradually slowed down. Her wanderings brought her to deserted buildings, their occupants all attending the game. She peered into the small stone cells that served as sleeping quarters. Not homes as such, as most of their lives the people spent being outside. All they contained were a handful of pots and a raised end with light blankets where their owners slept. Rounding the next corner, she was met with a sight that horrified her. Cage after cage filled with birds captured for their astonishingly bright plumage. Hurriedly checking that no-one was around, she set about releasing the captives.

'Fly quietly my friends,' she said, as she let them go, 'or men will come.'

The birds cocked their heads to one side in understanding and flew away quietly. All except one, a quetzal. This bird perched on a nearby ledge, studying its saviour.

'You can talk to birds,' it said.

Ixchel turned to face it. 'Oh, you can understand me' she replied, 'I wasn't sure. A porcupine spoke to me once, but none since. I thought I may have imagined it.'

'It is a gift from Ek Balem. Use it wisely and keep it hidden from humans.'

'Why?'

'Because they would not understand and lack of understanding leads to mistrust.'

Young as she was, Ixchel knew what that meant.

The bird flew up, dropping a single red feather at her feet.

'My gift to you,' she called. 'My name is Quie. When you need my help, call and I will come.'

Ixchel gathered up the precious feather and hid it in an inside pocket of her tunic.

'Thank you, sister quetzal,' she called, her mind racing excitedly with this new knowledge.

Now that all the small cages were empty, her eyes alighted on a much larger cage hidden at the back. Its occupant lay curled up but sprang to its feet as she approached, staring aggressively at her and baring sharp teeth. With a new-found confidence from knowing that she would be understood, Ixchel spoke,

'Be still brother jaguar. I mean you no harm.'

The big cat held her gaze, assessing her and then slowly backed down. With trembling hands, Ixchel tried to undo the rope tying the cage door. The rope was coarse, and the knots pulled too tight for her small fingers. She reached for her small knife, only to remember that she had left it in her treasure basket, thinking that she wouldn't need it in the city. Again and again, she tried to loosen the rope until her fingers bled with the effort. She stood up and kicked the empty cages that she had opened so easily and stamped her feet. Her hands rested on her head, where her fingers caught on something sharp. Pulling the porcupine quill from her hair, she attacked the rope once more, using the quill to prise open the knots, forcing it in-between the fibres where her fingers couldn't fit, until eventually the rope came loose and the jaguar was free. He walked past her and disappeared quickly, seeking a way back to the rainforest. Ixchel sprinted after him, so eager to escape the confines of the city she completely forgot about her family.

Chapter Three

Lost

Eloy was totally engrossed in the pok-a-tok. Although he couldn't see a great deal of what was happening, the shouts and cheers of the crowd immersed him in the contest. A few times Hadwin had lifted the boy onto his shoulders, allowing him to peer above the heads of the other spectators and watch the athletes displaying their talents. The game was fast and furious, players using hips, wrists, elbows and knees with great skill to keep the hard rubber ball with their team. The king's men were painted in white spirals and wore their hair up and crested with feathers. The opposition had blue spirals on their chests. It was thrilling and played at express pace.

Perched up on his father's shoulders, Eloy inhaled the atmosphere. Shouts, cheers, and excitement surrounded him. Suddenly he sensed another emotion, fear. Puzzled, he stared into the crowd trying to pinpoint its source. All he could feel was the excitement. He shook the feeling away and returned his attention to the game.

'What will the winners get?' he asked Hadwin.

'They will receive gifts and honours from the king.'

'And the losers?'

'They will be sacrificed. King Cadmael has already taken their city. Playing this game is their way to gain honour before the gods.'

Eloy went quiet, contemplating this darker side of the day's entertainment, but despite knowing this the thrill of the competition engulfed him. The match lasted most of the day. The opposition had scored highly but the king's men sealed victory by passing the ball through one of the stone circles which gave them an instant win. The spectators went wild, cheering, clapping and shouting the king's name.

King Cadmael stood to acknowledge his players who each bowed low. The losing team were escorted from the court by palace guards to await their fate. Once again Eloy felt the cold hand of fear around his heart. This time he knew where it came from. *Why am I feeling their emotions?* he wondered. Then he dismissed it as merely his mind thinking about what would happen to the losers.

'I want to be a pok-a-tok player when I'm older,' he said.

'My boy you were born a farmer and farmers do not play the king's game,' said Hadwin.

'But I am not like the other boys. I am stronger, faster. I know that I can play this game.'

Not wanting to spoil their day with an argument, Hadwin merely shrugged and said, 'We'll see. Now where is your sister?'

It was only then that they all realised that Ixchel was not with them. They had all been so caught up in the day's entertainment none of them had noticed that she was gone.

'I thought she was with you,' said Abha, 'when she left my side.'

'And I thought she was with you.'

'She is so small,' said Abha. 'She will be frightened. Eloy, have you seen her?'

'No, Mother. I was too busy watching the game. I should have held her hand.'

'It's not your fault.'

'She can't be far. Let the crowd disperse a little and then it will be easier to look for her,' said Hadwin, trying to contain his worry.

Eloy scanned the faces, but nowhere could he find any sign of Ixchel. The more he gazed at the throng of people, the less he saw. Everything became a jumble of legs, arms and colour. Unable to discern anything clearly, he sat on a low stone wall and closed his eyes. A tumult of voices filled his head, snatches of conversation from each passing group. His parents were frantically asking people if they had seen a young girl, their hands held at chest height to indicate her size. Each appeal was met with a negative. In amongst the noise and clamour Eloy felt the anxiety and uncertainty in his parents; felt it as strongly as he felt his own emotion. The overwhelming desire to find their child coursed through his parent's veins like oxygen. Somehow, he had a window into their hearts. *It's because we are all so worried, that's all,* he thought. Before he had time to dwell on it, Hadwin snatched his hand and pulled him roughly to his feet.

'We have to go my son. She is clearly not here. We will scour the nearby pathways. She won't have gone far.'

Despite his father's words, Eloy could see the worry imprinted on his father's face. He too was deeply uneasy. Ixchel was only comfortable in the rainforest, this city did not suit her at all. In his mind he pictured her cowering in a doorway, alone, frightened. *Why didn't I watch her more closely? Why was I so engrossed in the game? I knew she didn't want to be here.*

The three of them walked down every pathway, looked in every doorway, asked every vendor, stopped passers-by going about their business, but no-one recalled seeing a young girl on her own. The sun was sinking below the horizon when they rounded a corner to a great commotion. Eloy watched a group being berated by a man standing in front of a stack of empty cages.

'Who has done this?' the man shouted. 'Which one of you has ruined my trade? This is theft. I will report you all to the guards.'

Not wanting to get involved in a local dispute, Hadwin and Abha turned away, but something

drew Eloy to the scene and he slipped his father's hand and ran to take a closer look. The group looked as bewildered as the man himself.

'We were all at the game,' they said.

'None of us have been here today.'

'You must have left the cages open.'

This only further incensed the man. 'Do I look stupid? These cages were all closed and tied. Someone has opened them and freed all my birds and a jaguar. That was worth a lot of money. Now which of you was it?'

The arguments raged on as Eloy rejoined his parents.

'I think Ixchel was here,' he said to them.

'Then I must talk to them,' said Hadwin.

'No, Father. All of the man's birds have been released. I think she might have done it. I know she hates the cages.'

Hadwin looked at Abha. 'Come away,' she said. 'We don't want trouble.'

Reluctantly, Hadwin agreed. 'We don't know for sure that it was her. It is late. Maybe she found her way home. We can't do much more tonight, let's go.'

Eloy saw a frown crossing his father's brow. He knew what that meant. *I hope it wasn't you Ixchel,* he thought, *or father will be angry.* Hadwin strode off so fast that Abha and Eloy had to run to keep up. Very few of the morning's visitors remained, so exiting was much quicker than entering had been and they soon found themselves back at the farmer's settlement.

Heart pounding, Eloy hung back when his father entered their hut, waiting for the shouting to start but none did. Instead, Hadwin stepped back outside and shook his head at Abha whose face crumpled, the faint hope she had carried with her, that Ixchel would be at home, gone in an instant. Eloy was suddenly wrapped tightly in her arms until she composed herself and began gathering sticks for the fire, focusing on the mundane task of preparing supper to distract her frantic mind. Meanwhile Hadwin asked around the village in case Ixchel had come back with a neighbour.

Eloy and Hadwin, as per custom sat together to eat their stew. Abha sat outside with hers, but she couldn't eat, she was too worried. When the meal was finished, they came together to discuss what to do in the morning, where to look and who to ask about their missing child. The strain on his mother's face was obvious even in the dim light and Eloy knew that she wouldn't sleep that night. A barely audible rustle made him turn to see Ixchel standing in the doorway. Jumping to his feet, he shouted, 'She's here,' and he dragged her into the room.

'Ixchel, where have you been? We… we thought you were lost,' sobbed Abha, scooping her daughter into her arms.

'I was here,' said Ixchel. 'I didn't like the city, so I came home.'

'On your own?' said Abha.

'You should have stayed with us,' said Hadwin. 'We have been searching for you for hours.'

'You were all watching the game. I was bored and…'

'And left without any consideration for us,' said Hadwin, his face reddening with anger. 'What have you been doing all day?'

'I… I have been foraging in the rainforest. Look, I found papaya.'

'The rainforest. The rainforest,' raged Hadwin. 'How many times have you been told not to go in there alone especially after sunset. There are jaguars in there.'

Ixchel, defiant now, said, 'They won't hurt me. I set one free this afternoon.'

'So, it was you that released that man's creatures?'

'They shouldn't be in cages.'

This last remark was too much for Hadwin. He seized her by the arms and pushed her into the corner of the room where he proceeded to yell at her about respecting other people's property and not bringing shame onto the family by her reckless actions. Despite the verbal scouring, Ixchel refused to cry, squeezing her eyes tight to prevent the tears from flowing.

When Hadwin had finished, Ixchel crawled over to the corner of the hut where the children slept and covered herself in a blanket.

'You are not allowed into the rainforest anymore, do you hear. It is time you learnt the ways of the women so that you can become a good wife and a proper member of this community.'

Hadwin stormed out of the hut to calm down. Abha busied herself cleaning pots. Eloy looked to her mother to intervene, but Abha shook her head, knowing that this wasn't the time. He tiptoed over to his sister, crept under the blanket, cradling her to him. Too upset to share the secret of her interaction with the animals, she let him hold her, while her sobs finally came.

Chapter Four

First Meeting

In the morning, Eloy and his father left early to go hunting. Abha and Ixchel had a day in the maize fields ahead of them. It was common for the women to tend to the crops but Ixchel had rarely assisted her mother, always running off instead. Until now, Abha had indulged her youngest twin. The events in the city had changed that. It had been made very clear to Ixchel that she must learn the ways of the women and not play in the rainforest. Knowing that protesting wasn't going to get her anything except another telling off,

Ixchel acquiesced, hoping that a few days of humbly obeying her parents would earn her a reprieve.

The women busied themselves removing weeds, insects and any dead leaves from the crop; tending to the plants with as much care as if they were babies. Ixchel realised that unlike the other village girls who worked with their mothers, she was nothing but a hindrance to hers. She inadvertently pulled up the wrong plants, played with the insects and was constantly distracted by birds flying overhead or the occasional iguanodon that had strayed into the fields, sitting down to talk to it, trying out her extraordinary gift to make sure she still had it.

Much of the talk amongst the women was about their husbands or gossip about who was to be betrothed to whom, who was pregnant and upcoming celebrations. Most of it drifted by Ixchel, melting into a persistent hum. It was only when she heard her name mentioned that she paused to listen. Two of the older girls were talking about her.

'That's Ixchel,' said the first, pointing in her direction. 'Looks like her mother is finally trying to turn her into something marriageable.'

'No-one's going to want her. Look how ugly she is with her round forehead.'

'It does look strange,' agreed the first one.

'I've heard she's not right in the head.'

'Yes, and lazy too, never helps her family. They must be so embarrassed, especially Eloy. Imagine having that for a sister. No wonder he tries to pretend that they are not related.'

This last remark was too much for Ixchel and she flew at the speaker, pulling her hair, knocking her to the ground then straddling her body shouting, 'Take that back,' while pummelling her victim.

The second girl ran to her mother who hurried up, dragging Ixchel away.

'What is going on?' shouted Abha seeing her daughter being restrained.

'She was saying mean things about me and us,' said Ixchel.

The girl she had hit looked up and said, 'Nothing that isn't true. Look at you, hissing and spitting like a wild cat. I feel sorry for your mother.'

This infuriated Ixchel even more and she writhed and wrenched in her captor's arms.

'Enough, Ixchel,' said Abha, pulling her away, pinching her arms sharply. 'Go home.'

'But she deserved it,' protested Ixchel.

'Just go. Go!'

Ixchel ran, leaving Abha to smooth things over with the other women. Instead of making for the hut she sprinted into the rainforest losing herself in the undergrowth, hot tears of anger streaming down her face. Deeper and deeper, she ran, driven by anger and wanting to put as much space as possible between herself and the village. The rainforest, sensing her unhappiness, wrapped itself around her, a green comfort blanket. It guided her, pulling her unwittingly down unknown pathways where the foliage was denser and the light barely filtered through the thick branches above her. Dark green fronds towered over her, closing around. The atmosphere was stifling and her back itched from the sweat trickling down in the heat. The only sound was the noise of her feet rustling in the fallen leaves. No bird song or hum of insects reached her ears. Silence enveloped her. She stopped; aware, from the prickling on the back of her neck, that she was being watched. Warm breath. Whose? A rush of air above her alerted her to the movement of her pursuer and then she was staring into the eyes of a huge black jaguar. She didn't flinch, holding her ground with as much poise as she could muster.

'You have grown strong, little girl,' said the jaguar, circling her on giant paws.

Ixchel watched them warily, knowing that one blow from them would kill her.

'I have been watching you carefully.'

'How do you know me, brother jaguar?' she asked.

'I am Ek Balem, God of Darkness. It was I who breathed life into you when you were born.'

'Then I thank you Lord Balem,' she said, unsure what else to say. 'My mother often talks of the miracle of my survival. Does she know that it was your doing?'

'How could she? But your parents did make many offerings to thank me and for that, I am grateful.'

Ek Balem studied her, 'You saved one of my kin, thank you. Too many of us are hunted by your king so that he can adorn himself in our pelts and claim himself all-powerful.' While he spoke, he prowled noiselessly around her, noting the strength in her limbs and the tautness of her muscles. She felt like he was sizing her up for dinner.

'Are…are you going to eat me?' she managed to blurt out.

This remark was greeted by a low rumbling sound and she realised that he was laughing.

'Child, if I was going to eat you, I would have killed you with one blow before you were aware that I was behind you.'

Ixchel shivered at the thought.

'You are under my protection and no rainforest creature will attack you. Humans, however, I cannot protect you from.'

Ixchel thought of the telling off that she knew awaited her when she got back and felt the humiliation from the last one and wondered if she should simply stay here.

Ek Balem read her thoughts, 'You must go back. Obey your parents and come to the rainforest only at night and only under a crescent moon. It is only on those nights that you will be able to get away unseen.'

'Did you make me able to talk with the animals?'

'You have discovered that ability then. You are one of mine, it is part of who you are. Have you told anyone else?'

'Only Eloy, but I am not sure that he really believed me.'

'Tell no-one else and take care that you are not found out.'

She made to speak, but he raised a paw to silence her.

'Do as I ask. Soon I will call you to me again. Your brother too. Until then, be the dutiful daughter your parents want. Trust only Eloy, he alone understands you.'

With one bound he was gone, leaving her alone, bewildered and lost. Something moved on the ground hidden by the debris of the rainforest floor. Ixchel watched until she knew what approached, then pounced, grabbing the snake behind its head and lifting it from the undergrowth. Their eyes locked but Ixchel remained aware of its tail attempting to wrap itself around her legs and constrict them. Her left hand snatched it and the snake found itself dangling at arm's length from her body.

'Brother Kingsnake, I mean you no harm, but I am lost and need a guide to see me home. Will you be that guide?'

The snake writhed angrily in her hands, its blue-black scales shimmering in the narrow shafts of sunlight filtering through the foliage. Ixchel's grip was far tighter than her small hands suggested. The snake fought and fought against her until, exhausted from the effort, it finally gave in.

'Since I have been unable to free myself I will guide you back, but only if you can keep hold of my tail.'

Ixchel pondered this bargain, knowing that the snake would use all his wiles to make her let go in revenge for his humiliation; crawling through spaces that she could not easily follow.

'I am lost therefore I take your offer,' she said, releasing the snake's head whilst retaining her grip on its tail. Exactly as she expected, the snake slithered quickly away, pulling her through the undergrowth at surprising speed. He crawled under sharp thorns that ripped at her skin even as she lay flat on her belly to pass beneath them. On they went, through mud pools edged with animal droppings. He found slimy ponds and pulled her into the shallows, filling her nostrils with the rancid smell of rotting vegetation. From time to time, he would pause and turn to look at her smothered in filth, revelling in her discomfort, before moving on. When the stench and muck failed to loosen her grip, he tried another tactic. This time he pulled her through an anthill so angering the inhabitants that they crawled over her biting every piece of flesh they could find. The pain from so many bites was excruciating but even that could not make her let go of his tail.

When the trees around her were familiar, Ixchel did let go expecting the snake to disappear back to his domain, instead he slithered round to face her.

'Sister, you have proved your bravery and determination and for that I honour you. My name is Nitor and we will meet again.'

And then he was gone, leaving Ixchel bewildered, *'Had she just undergone some sort of test? What did he mean, we will meet again?* It had been an afternoon of strange events. The stench of the slime oozing down her tunic and arms made her wretch now that she was still enough to really smell it. The cuts and bruises and bites that she had endured also began to itch or hurt. *I must find a cenote,* she thought. These large underground freshwater pools gave the villagers their water. Not wanting to wash her filth off in a cenote used for drinking, she took herself off to another site she knew. The one she wanted was her and Eloy's secret pool. They often snuck away here in the hot summer days to cool off, enjoying the freedom of swimming undisturbed amongst the blind black fish that inhabited the water.

The entrance was down a hidden tunnel carved into the rock by years of rainwater seeping through it. The way in was masked by tall bracken fronds, easily missed by the unaware. Ixchel, with her senses tuned into the rainforest, could taste the moisture in the air drifting up from the underground pool. Pulling aside the bracken, she began the slippery descent to the cenote. Down and down, she went, the light dimming with every footstep. The increasing drip drip of the water through the rock told her she was almost at the pool. Usually, she and Eloy would have to feel their way over the last few metres but today she found her eyes could see clearly in the dark and wondered at this new skill that allowed her to stride forward confidently to where the tunnel opened out into a vast underground cavern filled with fresh water. An opening in the roof let in just enough light to see by. Shadows played on the walls and sparkles of light danced on the centre of the pool. It was a magical and calm place. Ixchel relaxed, wading into the water, letting it wash away the slime and mess; the coolness of the water easing the pain and irritation of her bites and bruises. The small black fish swam around her, the brave ones getting close enough to tickle her feet. A cool peacefulness washed over her. The cave was a haven and with each stroke her strength was renewed. Sometimes she would dive under and see if she could touch the bottom but to no avail, sometimes she just lay on her back floating with the fish until the darkening sky warned her it was time to go home. Reluctantly, after swimming to the shore, she stepped out to wend her way back up the tunnel leaving a watery trail in her wake.

Although evening was descending it was still very warm, which meant that her thin tunic soon dried, her hair too. By the time she reached home she was clean and dry. Luckily, she was back first and busied herself lighting the cooking fire, sweeping the floor and generally making herself useful.

Voices outside alerted her to the arrival of the hunters. Nervously stepping outside, she watched the men and boys return with many agoutis, the large gopher-like rodents that roamed the rainforest and made good eating. In the centre of the group, men were carrying the carcass of a large deer and Eloy, his face marked with blood was being carried triumphantly on Hadwin's shoulders. Seeing her there, Hadwin called out.

'Ixchel, your brother has proven himself a true hunter. See what prize he has killed for us.'

Ixchel looked from the deer to her brother's proud face and her blood ran cold. *How could he have done this? He has never killed before. Trapped yes; but never killed.* His demeanour was changed too. *Is that really my brother, revelling in the taking of a life even if it is for food?*

The troop of men passed. She went back inside to await Abha's return from the fields and the consequences she knew that she must face.

Fortunately, Abha had calmed down over the afternoon and when she saw the effort Ixchel had made to prepare the meal, she refrained from shouting at her.

'Thank you, Ixchel, I can see that you have been busy.'

Ixchel touched her mother's hand. 'I'm sorry that I embarrassed you today. But they were saying such mean things about me.'

'Gossip can be unpleasant child, but there are other ways to challenge people on it. I'm afraid your violent reaction only served to confirm their opinions.'

'I know,' said Ixchel quietly. 'Will you tell father?'

'I haven't decided,' said Abha, but when Hadwin and Eloy returned they were in such good spirits that she didn't want to ruin their day by mentioning their wayward daughter's transgressions.

Thankful to have escaped further punishment, Ixchel spent the evening listening quietly to Hadwin lauding his boy the hunter, explaining how Eloy had stalked the deer on silent feet and then thrown his spear with such accuracy and strength it had killed the deer instantly.

'When I have mastered the bow too, I will be the best hunter in all the villages.'

'That you will my son, that you will,' said Hadwin, bursting with pride.

A growing weariness settled on Ixchel and she crept quietly away to bed to reflect on the day's events and what they meant for the future. She wanted so badly to talk to Eloy about her meeting with Lord Balem and being able to talk with the animals and see in the dark, but he was too full of the day's glory.

'Ixchel, I was so much better than the other hunters. You should have seen me. I outran them and my traps were so well-set, catching agouti was as easy as picking fruit off a tree. And then the deer. I was so silent even you would not have heard me.'

She smiled weakly at her brother. All this talk of hunting upset her even though she knew they needed the meat to feed the village. For once, Eloy failed to notice her discomfort, letting his tongue run away with tales of his success.

When he finally finished, he looked at her expectantly. 'Say you're pleased with my skill,' he said.

'Yes brother. I am always pleased for you when you do things well but perhaps you enjoyed the kill a bit too much.'

'What do you mean?'

'You took an animal's life, even if it will feed the village. You shouldn't be pleased about that.'

'Why do you say that?'

'Because I can talk to them. I told you, remember.'

'Yes, you told me you spoke to a porcupine, but when we tried with the lizard I just got bitten.'

'I know, but yesterday, in the city, I spoke with a quetzal bird and a jaguar and today I met Ek Balem himself. I was so scared Eloy but he told me the animal speech is part of me. Isn't that amazing. Maybe it's part of you too.'

Eloy stared at her, 'Why would the jaguar lord choose to meet you and not me,' he found himself saying.

'I don't know but it was so amazing and frightening at the same time, and I can see in the dark too.' She grabbed his hand, 'Isn't it wonderful.'

But Eloy remained silent, the cold hand of jealousy, wrapping itself around his heart.

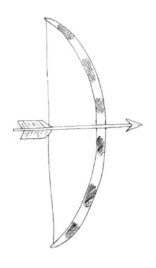

Chapter Five

Jealousy

The next day Eloy was up very early. Ixchel's revelations had not sat well with him. He wanted to be pleased for her, he did, so why wasn't he? Grabbing his sling and some clay balls he headed to the edge of the village. Shortly after, Ixchel found him destroying a large water pot in a frenetic hail of sling shots.

'Brother, why are you so angry with that pot?'

He turned to face her, sling loaded and ready. Instinctively she ducked as he took aim only for him to drop his arms in horror at the last moment as he realised what he had been about to do.

'Ixchel, I'm sorry. I'm sorry.'

She glared at him; teeth bared; a palpable wall of tension between them. A large iguana, witnessing the scene, suddenly ran behind Eloy, snatching the sling out of his hand and running off into the trees with it.

'Hey,' shouted Eloy, indignantly. Then turned back to see Ixchel doubled up with laughter. 'Did you tell it to do that?'

'No', she laughed, 'but you should see your face.'

Eloy tried to remain indignant but Ixchel's laughter was infectious and he too began to chuckle.

Harmony restored, they gathered up the pieces of pottery and began digging a hole to bury them.

'So it's true, you really can talk with the forest animals.'

'Yes, but it's a secret. Ek Balem said I was to tell no-one.'

'Except me?'

'You are my twin, of course I would tell you. He said I could trust you.'

'What was it like, being in front of a god?'

Ixchel thought for a moment, she had hardly given herself time to reflect on the meeting. 'I was terrified at first. He came as a black jaguar and he was so huge. And his paws.' She held her hands up in front of her to indicate the size. 'I could feel his breath; and his eyes, they were deep, really deep. I'm sure he looked into my soul.'

Eloy shivered, 'I'm not sure I would like that.'

'But then he began speaking and somehow I felt calmer.'

'I wonder why you got his gift and not me, after all I am the eldest,' said Eloy, feeling a pang of jealousy again. 'And I'm a boy.'

Ixchel laughed again, 'Oh Eloy, as if that would make a difference to a god.'

'Don't mock me,' he said.

'I'm not, but you shouldn't assume that you are more deserving than me just because I am a girl. Besides, I'm the one that loves the rainforest the most and I was the one that set the birds and the jaguar free. You prefer the city to the forest anyway.'

'That might be true, but it's still not fair that you get a special gift and not me,' he said petulantly.

'Maybe you did,' said Ixchel.

'What do you mean?'

'Your speed, your strength, your hunting skills. They might be your gift.'

Eloy shrugged and kicked the dirt. 'I am good because I practise and practise and practise, Ixchel. And I do as I am told by father when he teaches me about farming and hunting. That's why I am good. And I want to be a king's warrior one day, so I have to work on my skills.'

He scuffed the ground one more time then sprinted away, leaving Ixchel wondering what had just happened between them.

'He said he would send for you,' she called after him, but he was too far away to hear her. She wandered back home where Abha was waiting for her.

'Come daughter we have maize to grind, it has been soaking all night, now we must make the dough for the tortillas.'

'Yes, mother,' said Ixchel. 'I will fetch the metate from inside.'

If Abha was surprised at this lack of resistance to daily chores, she didn't show it. Ixchel came out of the hut having retrieved the metate, the large flat grinding stone. Abha placed some of the soaked maize in the centre and then showed Ixchel how to use a small oval stone to crush the kernels. While Ixchel worked on the maize, Abha made the atole porridge which they had for breakfast. Hadwin and Eloy ate theirs quickly, anxious to get to their work in the fields so that they could finish early.

'You are in a rush this morning, husband,' remarked Abha.

'We have a lot of work to do today; the fields, the weapons and cleaning the deer skin.'

Ixchel looked up from her grindstone at this, but Eloy would not look directly at her, instead focusing on his breakfast. After they left, Ixchel and Abha spent a pleasant morning engaged in domestic chores before heading to the maize fields in the afternoon. This time Ixchel ignored the gossip, staying close to her mother's side at all times. When the comments got too much, she balled her hands into fists and punched the ground, filling her head with Ek Balem's voice telling her to behave.

That evening Eloy was in a buoyant mood. The members of the hunting party had praised his prowess all day and he relished in it, reporting back to his mother and sister all the things that had been said.

'I am pleased for you my son,' said Abha, 'and very proud.'

Ixchel nodded in agreement, chipping in with words of encouragement. When they retired to their sleeping area he was still talking.

'I am going to be the best hunter this village has ever seen.'

'I'm sure you are,' said Ixchel, 'but don't get too carried away with the idea of your success.'

'What does that mean?'

'Don't become arrogant brother. Remember to thank the gods for your skills.'

'My skills are my skills, gained by hard work and practice,' replied Eloy. 'I will thank the gods when they give me a gift like yours.'

Ixchel heard a deep roar when he uttered those words and felt a shift in the ether. None of the others reacted; they had not noticed.

'Be careful brother,' she muttered. 'Be careful.'

******

That day proved to be a turning point in their relationship. Ixchel continued to follow Ek

Balem's instructions, trying to turn herself into a dutiful daughter; performing her tasks if not well at least quietly and uncomplainingly. Abha was very pleased with this new version of Ixchel and hoped that it would last. Each evening, when the twins settled down, Eloy would tell her about his day working in the fields or practising spear-throwing with the other boys. He never asked her about hers and because she had no time to herself, the days being full of chores, she found that she had little to say anyway. She hoped things would change back. Once a small lizard found its way into their corner and she began talking with it. Eloy pretended not to notice and feigned disinterest when she tried to include him.

When his bow training began, things changed again. Now, when they settled down for the night Eloy fell straight to sleep, worn out by his day's activity. He proved to be a natural with the bow. His sharp eyesight meant his aim was true. Once he had mastered the basics, he set himself increasingly difficult challenges: firing from the trees; over greater distances; and, with the help of the other boys, who threw broken pots or clods of earth into the air; moving targets. He rose at dawn to practise his skills with spear and bow, sprinted across fields until exhausted to increase his fitness or swam in the cenote to build stamina. In the evenings he ate twice as much as before, often finishing Ixchel's food too. As his appetite grew so hers diminished, the confines of domesticity taking their toll on her free spirit. Eloy became more gregarious, revelling in the company of the older boys, testing his strength in wrestling competitions or running contests, which he always won.

'Your brother is growing tall and strong,' remarked Abha one day as they worked in the fields, 'Whereas you my daughter, seem hardly to grow at all.'

'Perhaps I am meant to be small,' said Ixchel, looking around at the other girls of a similar age who were nearly twice her size.

'You should eat more. I will prepare a special stew just for you.'

'Really mother, there is no need. I may be small but I am strong.' To demonstrate she gathered up a large bundle of maize stalks and carried them to the fire mound. Abha watched her fondly.

'You have become so helpful since you stopped running off to the forest every day,' she said when Ixchel returned to her place. She smiled at her daughter who managed a weak one in response and Abha could see that there was no light behind her daughter's eyes anymore. 'I'm sorry child that you are unhappy, but this is the way of things for us women.'

'I will get used to it, eventually,' said Ixchel, although she knew that she never would.

Chapter Six

Snakeskin

The days and years passed, Ixchel became more withdrawn, barely communicating, missing not only the rainforest but also her twin who hardly acknowledged her existence anymore.

Only with the waxing of the moon did the light flicker in her eyes. She completed her tasks thoroughly to avoid being asked to do them again. When the night came she would feign tiredness, going to her blanket early, lying quietly, waiting for Eloy to settle which he did quickly after his daily exertions. The slowing of his breathing was her cue to creep away to her beloved rainforest. It welcomed her warmly, surrounding her like a balm, nourishing her mind and soul. The trees bent their branches allowing her to climb amongst them and the nocturnal creatures sought her out. With the night vision of a cat, she was easily able to see her way. Here she felt alive and at home, at one with her surroundings; back in the village she felt shackled and a misfit.

One night, shaking off her gloom, she jumped down from the trees, wandering further into the rainforest. Something blue-black nestling in a tree root caught her eye.

'Master kingsnake, Nitor, is that you?' she asked, but the snake did not reply.

Puzzled, she gently touched the scales only to discover it was a discarded skin. *So, you were here,* she thought. *Well, I will keep your gift.* Picking up the skin, she wound it twice around her neck like a collar. Finding the snakeskin encouraged her to look more closely at the ground, moving catlike on all fours. Her shoulders, strong from swimming, carried her weight easily.

'Why do you move like that?' said a small voice behind her.

Glancing behind her, she saw Silas, the porcupine she had rescued.

'To observe the ground more clearly,' she replied, 'Which is a good thing.'

'Is it?' said Silas. 'That would depend if you are the hunter or the hunted.'

'How so?' said Ixchel, sitting back on her haunches.

'If you are hunting you have the advantage of seeing tracks but if you are the hunted, you present a larger target.'

'Who would hunt me?' she asked.

'Humans always hunt the exotic. Why do you think I keep my quills black and white?' he said, spreading them out to show her. 'If we showed our true colours, they would hunt my kind and put us in cages for their own amusement or pluck our quills to adorn their hair like they do with quetzal birds.'

'Your true colours?' said Ixchel. 'What colours should you be?'

He shuffled nearer. 'Tell no-one,' he said. 'Close your eyes tightly.' Ixchel did as she was told, Silas gently pricked her skin with a spine and then her mind filled with an image of the little creature, his spines a blaze of bright pink, tipped with purple.

'Oh, oh how beautiful,' she uttered, opening her eyes to see the little animal there, black and white as usual. 'No wonder you cover them up.'

'The king has many creatures in his palace, all in cages,' said Silas. 'Trophies to show his power. I do not wish to be one of them.'

'If I were ruler, I would release them all and make it a law that animals should not be caged. Then you could show whatever colours you want.'

'A noble wish, sister, but how can a farmer's daughter ever change things?' and he wandered off leaving Ixchel picturing his bright spines.

The first streaks of dawn edged over the horizon prompting her to turn hurriedly back home, aware that she was late. The early risers were emerging from their huts when she reached the settlement, so she had to dodge between the huts that formed the outer circle of the village to avoid being seen, working her way carefully to the centre of the village near the well where her family dwelt. Luckily, sleep still held on to them, a mantle yet to fall completely from their shoulders, so they failed to notice a young girl creeping through the village. Praying that no-one would be awake she tiptoed up to the house. To her dismay, Eloy was outside sharpening his spears.

'Where have you been?' he demanded.

'Walking.'

'Long walk', he said, towering over her, 'You've been gone all night.'

'I…I went to the rainforest. I had to get away.'

'It's forbidden. Why can't you ever be obedient? I will tell father.'

'Eloy please. No. It is alright for you. You have freedom to go where you please, the same as when we were small. I am tied to women's work.'

'Because you are a woman, or soon will be. We are twelve this summer and you must be married soon. It will be hard enough for mother to make a match with your strange looks. Don't make it any harder.'

Ixchel's hand automatically touched her round forehead, before she replied,

'What has happened to you? We used to be so close.'

'I have grown up. And I am to join the king's hunt today. If I do well our family will be rewarded. But not if you embarrass us,' he said, grabbing her shoulders.

'Don't Eloy. Don't hunt for the king. He is cruel.'

But Eloy was unmoved, pushing her to one side with a final warning, 'I will say nothing this time, but if you do it again, I will tell father. I will not let you disgrace this family again.' Gathering up his spears, bow and arrows, he marched off to the muster point in the centre of the village leaving Ixchel alone and bewildered by this new, hard-edged brother.

Creeping inside, she was pleased to see that her parents still slept. In her corner she took off the snakeskin, relieved that Eloy had been too angry to notice it, placing it in a small basket of possessions that she kept hidden in a hollow that she had dug into the ground and covered with a small woven mat.

'I must hide you,' she whispered to the skin, 'or my parents will take you.' With her treasure hidden, she busied herself making breakfast and fetching water so when her parents awoke, they found her busy with chores.

'It appears that our daughter is finally learning the proper ways,' said Hadwin. 'We may yet find her a husband.'

Abha wasn't so sure, but didn't want to voice her concerns, she could still sense the wildness in her daughter even if the child endeavoured to conceal it.

'Eloy,' called Hadwin, looking outside for him.

'He has already gone,' said Ixchel. 'He was up early too.'

'It is a big day for him, but he cannot do it on an empty belly,' said Hadwin. 'Give me some maize bread for him.' He grabbed a chunk and headed off to find his son, leaving the women to their tasks.

The king and his entourage arrived with enormous clamour. He wore the finest jaguar skins and the tallest headdress anyone had ever seen. Soldiers pushed anyone or anything out of the way to allow the king a clear path wherever he went. Messages had been sent out to the settlements prior to his arrival informing the villagers of the king's intention to hunt in their area of the rainforest. He demanded that each settlement send their best hunter to join his party.

Eloy saw them standing uncomfortably behind the soldiers.

The king stood, waiting to be presented with the last hunter. Eloy stepped forward.

'Do you mock me?' roared the king. 'What insult is this to send me a child?'

Knees shaking and head bowed, Hadwin spoke. 'Mighty king, do not be deceived by his age. My son is the best hunter in these parts.'

The other men nodded nervously. The king was unmoved, sending a soldier to examine the boy more closely. Eloy stood his ground, letting the older man feel his muscles and prod and poke him. 'His muscles are solid, your highness.'

The king signalled to a steward behind him. 'Release the birds.'

To the assembled village he said, 'If he can hit one of the birds, he may join us.'

A trio of mockingbirds took flight. Eloy whipped out his bow and three arrows and hit not one, but all three. Bowing low, he said, 'My king, I humbly ask that I be allowed to join your hunting party.'

Taken aback by his skill, but not wanting to show it, the king stared at the boy for several moments, appraising him and giving the appearance of deliberating before nodding and pointing to the group of hunters.

Eloy strode towards the other hunters, head held high. He knew that he deserved his place and now, so did they. With a nod to Hadwin, who was walking back into the group of villagers, Eloy took his place. The king signalled and the party moved on, his soldiers parting the way for him to pass. The large entourage entered the rainforest with such a commotion that birds and animals scattered in panic. The soldiers hacked their way through with no regard for the damage they caused. Nests fell from trees whose branches were viciously chopped to allow the king to pass beneath without damaging his headdress. Murmurs of disapproval rippled through the ranks of villagers at this wanton destruction. They all had more respect for the land. Eloy, was less horrified, still swelled with pride at passing the test to show off his skill.

When they reached a spot the King declared was suitable because of its proximity to a cenote, they set up camp. A priest in brightly coloured robes and wearing a tall, feathered headdress, stepped forward. He lit some copal incense and walked around the perimeter with it, blessing the cenote, the campsite and all the people. Servants materialised, removing King Cadmael's elaborate headgear and stowing it safely away. King Cadmael allowed the face painter to approach him. Clearly nervous, the man's hand shook as he applied paint under the eyes.

'Put it on smoothly, you idiot,' snapped King Cadmael, which only served to make the man more nervous.

'Go, go!' yelled King Cadmael. 'Send me someone competent. I must look fearsome if I am to hunt.'

A second man stepped forward. He applied the paint in quick smooth strokes, black and white stripes leading from the king's nose to the edge of his cheeks. When he had finished another servant rushed forward with a mirror. King Cadmael studied his reflection carefully while the face painter waited anxiously to one side. Sturdy moccasins were placed on his feet and a gilded spear was placed in his hand. The High Priest feigned shock and awe when he saw the king in his hunting garb.

'Mighty Ahaw, King, how terrible you look.'

'Do you think so?' said King Cadmael, still admiring his reflection.

'Yes Ahaw. You will strike fear into the hearts of the beasts that you hunt.'

'It is very important that I do.'

Those around the king nodded their approval, some even shielded their eyes in an attempt to appear afraid, a gesture that pleased him. Satisfied at last, with his preparations, Cadmael dropped the mirror and called his hunters.

'Today we will hunt in three groups. Find me the best quetzal birds, the largest deer and enough agouti to fill the royal kitchens for a moon.'

Again, Eloy heard the men muttering.

'If we kill that much what will be left for us?'

'That is too much. We should only kill what we need.'

But the king heard none of this, he cared little for the needs of others. He continued,

'I will lead one party, my captain another, and the priest the third.'

He wandered amongst the village hunters picking his group which naturally involved the biggest and strongest of the men. Eloy puffed out his chest and stood as tall as he could make himself, hoping to be noticed. It worked. The king paused in front of him.

'You, boy. You will join me. We shall see if your earlier success was merely a fluke.'

Eloy bowed and fell into line. Once the king had finished choosing his group, they set off. Eloy was the first to pick up tracks.

'Deer passed through here recently, Majesty.'

'Where did they go?'

Eloy pointed the way, but despite their skill the size of the hunting party made too much noise, so they were unable to get close enough to catch any deer. Snares were set for agouti instead, using berries to entice the animals out of the undergrowth. Another hunter reported seeing more deer up ahead. The group followed as stealthily as possible. Eloy watched them go, knowing that the deer would easily pick up on their approach. He peeled away to follow a new set of prints. On his own he was able to move silently. In a short time, he found himself face-to-face with a large stag, the two of them staring at each other for a brief moment before the stag darted away. Eloy was quicker. His first arrow pierced the animal's back leg, slowing it down. His second brought it to the ground and the third killed it.

To bring his prize back to the king, he cut down some large palm leaves to weave into a mat. When it was finished, he rolled the carcass onto it then lashed vines around and under the mat to begin the slow and arduous journey back to camp hauling the deer behind him. It was dark when he got back. King Cadmael was in a foul mood. Not only had his party failed to catch a deer, but the other groups had all caught more agouti, birds and ducks than his men too.

'Priest,' he called. 'We must make a sacrifice. I will not have my group outhunted. Priest!'

The priest rushed up, hurriedly fitting his headdress.

'Yes, Ahaw, Great one. What should we sacrifice, an agouti? A pigeon?'

'A man, you oaf. Find me a man.'

The priest cast about for a suitable specimen.

'The boy,' said the king, irritably. 'We will sacrifice the boy. Where is he?'

The priest and soldiers stood around muttering. None of them had seen him or thought about him since the morning. One of the soldiers tentatively stepped forward.

'He ... he is not here. Perhaps he ran home.'

King Cadmael was not pleased. 'Fetch the hunters. All of them.'

When the men were lined up the king paced up and down examining each of them in turn, then stopped in front of the biggest and strongest of them.

'You,' said the king, snapping his fingers. 'You will make an excellent offering.'

A pair of burly soldiers grabbed the unfortunate hunter by the arms and dragged him away to where the priest was preparing a sacrificial altar.

While all of this was taking place, Eloy staggered, exhausted, into the camp, pulling his trophy behind him. Most of the camp's inhabitants were waiting to witness the sacrifice so did not notice him. However, one sharp-eyed soldier had seen him approaching and ran off to tell the king.

'M…Majesty,' he stuttered, breathing heavily. King Cadmael, who was about to signal for the sacrifice to be made was not pleased at the interruption.

'The boy, Majesty. He has returned, with a deer.'

'Show me,' snapped the king.

The soldier led the way back to Eloy, now sitting casually on a log, the deer at his feet. He jumped up as the king approached, then bowed low.

'You killed this?' said the king.

'Yes, Majesty,' said Eloy.

'By yourself?'

'Yes.'

The other hunters, who had followed behind, shuffled nervously, waiting the king's response. He was quiet for several minutes, then he burst out laughing.

'Excellent young man. Excellent. See what a great hunter I chose. Priest, cancel the sacrifice,' he ordered, clapping his hands twice. 'My group has not been outhunted after all. Cooks, prepare the fire. We will eat well tonight.'

Chapter Seven

The King's Hunter

The rest of the evening passed calmly; King Cadmael's mood much brighter.

The hunter scheduled for sacrifice sat beside Eloy as they ate, quizzing him about how he had caught the deer.

'Stealth,' said Eloy. 'A large group could never be quiet enough and create too much scent.'

The big man nodded. 'Still, you must have quick reflexes. Deer are easily spooked.'

'It is so much easier on my own, but I couldn't say that to the king, so I snuck off.'

The big man smiled, 'Courage and skill. You are blessed indeed.'

Eloy wondered if the man was sincere, his instincts told him that he was.

In the morning, the king sent for Eloy. Two guards roughly escorted him, unhappy that this young boy was getting the king's attention.

'The deer you caught yesterday,' said the king, beckoning him forward. 'Can you catch me another?'

'Yes, Majesty,' said Eloy, bowing low.

'Good. Guards, I will be hunting with this boy. Keep your distance and do not disturb us.'

King Cadmael clicked his fingers and servants appeared instantly. Eloy watched in wonder as the king's attendants removed his headdress and robes, daubed his face in red paint and clothed him in a simple loin cloth and moccasins.

'Now boy,' he said, his change complete, 'Let's hunt. Find me the deer.'

Eloy wasn't at all sure that he would be successful with the king and his guards in tow even if they were following at a discreet distance, but he strode off confidently. Surprisingly, Eloy discovered that away from his entourage King Cadmael moved very quietly and they were soon able to track a small herd of deer. In his eagerness for the kill, the king pushed passed Eloy too carelessly and noisily. Alerted by the sound, the deer raised their heads, sniffed the air and dashed away. Cadmael's mood immediately changed; he uttered several oaths and then blamed Eloy for spooking them.

When he calmed down, they moved on. Eloy tracked more deer which Cadmael also spooked when he rushed to throw his spear. This happened repeatedly, each time the king's temper became more violent, slashing at the trees and destroying termite mounds. When he came across a snake basking in the afternoon sun, he grabbed it and threw it against a tree, killing it instantly.

The next time they came across deer, the king told Eloy to throw first. Not wanting to risk the deer escaping and enraging the king further, Eloy threw his spear with such accuracy, he killed a deer instantly. As it fell the king's spear landed in its side.

Eloy watched in disbelief as the king stepped forward, yanked the boys spear from the body, flinging it aside then calling, 'Men, Men. Come and retrieve my kill.'

Half a dozen guards appeared.

'See what a fine hunter I am,' he said, indicating the deer. 'An instant kill. Your king has true aim.'

The soldiers all applauded. Eloy, knowing better than to contradict his king, retrieved his spear, taking care to clean it before the soldiers could notice the blood.

The deer was carried back to camp where it was prepared and eaten. Nothing was said to Eloy, who the king had completely forgotten about, regaling his soldiers with his hunting prowess and basking in his glory. No-one dared to mention the second spear wound on the deer, fearing the consequences of King Cadmael's wrath if they dared to question it.

Back at the camp Eloy scuttled off to the other hunters, grabbing a meagre supper before laying down to sleep.

The next five days followed the same pattern. He was roughly awoken at dawn, escorted to the king and then the two of them hunted throughout the day. Eloy tracked and killed many many deer, more than the camp could possibly eat. King Cadmael claimed each kill as his own.

'That boy is the best hunter I have ever seen,' muttered a soldier to his neighbour. Unfortunately for him, the king overheard.

'What did you say?' demanded King Cadmael, turning on the soldier.

'N...n...nothing Ahaw,' he replied trembling.

King Cadmael stepped up to the man and yanked him by the hair. 'I know what I heard. Take him, tie him to that tree,' he said, pointing to one that was adjacent to a termite mound. The other soldiers did as they were told. When he was secured, the king destroyed the mound leaving the furious creatures to crawl all over the poor unfortunate man.

'Does anyone else care to question whether I am the greatest hunter?'

All the soldiers shook their heads. 'Good. Let the hunt continue.'

Eloy was appalled to see such a punishment.

On the evening of the seventh day, the king announced that it was to be the last and he would be returning to the city the following morning. Eloy was greatly relieved to hear this, having witnessed close hand the king's cruelty and bloodlust and grown mighty weary of it. He lay at the base of a tree under his blanket, gazing up at the waxing moon and felt a sudden longing for Ixchel. *Sister, I have not been kind to you,* he thought.

A leaf brushed his face, then another. A twig hit him. He stared up into the tree. A pair of dark eyes gazed back at him. He thought it was a cat at first but then realised that it was Ixchel perched on a branch above him. He climbed up to sit next to her.

'What are you doing here? This is no place for girls.'

'I missed you,' she said. 'And I wanted to see the king. Which I did. I sat in a tree right above him and he had no idea I was there.'

'No!' said Eloy, grabbing her hand. 'He is dangerous. What if you had been seen?'

'I wasn't,' she chuckled, then stiffened. 'Someone's coming. I'd better go.'

Two guards approached, 'Hunter boy,' they called, kicking his blanket. 'The king needs you.'

Eloy dropped to the ground. 'I thought the hunting was finished,' he said.

The guards laughed, 'Do you think the king is satisfied with deer? Tonight, we hunt jaguar.'

A barely stifled exclamation came from the branch.

'Who's there?' shouted the guard.

'No-one,' said Eloy. It's probably a bat. There was no sign of Ixchel, she had melted back into the rainforest without a sound.

'Let me gather my bow and spear,' said Eloy, scanning the ground for footprints that he could scrub out before the guards saw them. The only prints he could see were pawprints heading away from camp. Had a jaguar already been near? He reached for his spear, bending down to take a closer look at the ground.

'You won't need your weapons tonight,' said a guard, losing patience and hustling him along.

'But how will I hunt?' said Eloy.

The guards simply laughed at his question.

The King was growing impatient when they arrived.

'Boy, you have made yourself useful, but while we hunted my men have been laying traps. Tonight, we will take jaguar. He paused to adjust his cloak. 'Have you ever caught a jaguar before?'

Eloy shook his head.

'As you can see,' said King Cadmael, indicating the skins he was draped in, 'I have caught many. It is the king's prerogative to wear these pelts and show my subjects what a strong ruler I am.' He sneered at Eloy like he was a worm to be trodden on.

'I can see how mighty you are Majesty', said Eloy.

'Yes indeed,' said King Cadmael, 'but do you know what is mightier than these hides?'

Eloy shook his head, trying not to look the king in the eye.

'The skin of a black jaguar. I have heard a rumour of one being seen in these parts.'

Eloy looked up at this remark.

'So you have heard it too. Tell me what you know.'

Eloy said nothing.

'Tell me,' ordered the king.

Eloy mumbled something.

'Speak up, boy.'

'Some say that the jaguar god, Ek Balem, walks this part of the forest in the form of a black jaguar,' said Eloy, 'but I don't think that you can catch a god.'

'It is not up to you to think what I can or cannot do,' roared Cadmael. 'If such a jaguar exists then I will have it.'

He smiled at Eloy, 'Tonight, you will prove your true worth.'

Eloy had no idea how he was to accomplish this. Jaguars were secretive, their senses highly tuned and their paws lethal.

The king laughed at him.

'Don't worry boy, I don't expect you to track one down for me. It will track you. You are the bait.'

Eloy's bewilderment deepened as laughter rang out around him, the guards appreciating the joke of the king's chosen hunter now being hunted.

'Prepare him,' ordered the king. 'For I will have jaguar, black or mottled.'

The captain of the guards took Eloy to the offal pit, where the discarded bits of the deer carcasses lay and began smearing him in blood and hanging pieces of rancid meat around his neck.

'Why…why me?' asked Eloy. 'I thought the king was pleased with my hunting skills.'

The captain felt a pang of sorrow for this young naïve boy.

'You did too well,' he said. 'The king can't risk you returning to your village and telling everyone that you outhunted him.'

'I wouldn't,' said Eloy.

'Maybe not,' said the captain, 'but the king will not take that chance.'

He took Eloy back to the king who recoiled at the stench coming off him. A clap of his hands and Eloy found himself being pushed into the rainforest ahead of a small hunting party. The soldiers had dug a deep pit which they quickly located. Eloy was told to lie on the ground, perched precariously at the edge. The opening was then disguised with palm leaves.

'Lie still, boy,' said a soldier. 'Your scent will draw out the cats. If you run, I will spear you myself.'

The rest of the hunters and the king smeared themselves with animal excrement to disguise their own scent, then retired a short distance to watch and wait.

Eloy, alone and terrified, prayed to the gods for a quick end, fearing more than anything a slow mauling.

The night dragged on. Bats flew amongst the trees and possums snuffled about but there was no sign of the big cats. A couple of snakes came to investigate but not a single jaguar appeared.

By morning King Cadmael was incandescent with rage.

'Never has this happened!' he yelled. 'Never! Not in all the hunts I have been on have I failed to trap a single jaguar.'

The hunters stood around nervously.

'Guards, seize all of the hunters. They will be punished for this.'

The miserable hunters in the king's group were tied up and marched back to camp to await their fate.

'What of the boy, oh great one?' asked the captain.

The king shot a disdainful glance in Eloy's direction.

'It is his doing. Push him into the pit. He will die soon enough.'

The order was given, and two soldiers lifted Eloy and slung him into the pit where he landed awkwardly on his shoulder and banged his head on a rock, crying out in pain. The last thing he heard before he blacked out was the guard's laughter.

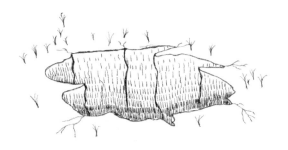

Chapter Eight

Rescue

King Cadmael and his entourage returned to the city with their prisoners, not caring for the mess they left behind. Those hunters fortunate enough to escape before they were rounded up ran back to their homes, praying that the guards would not come to their villages to look for them. Some stopped at other settlements on the way to pass on news of the missing ones, although all they really knew was that the king had taken them prisoner. One of them passed through Eloy's village and told Hadwin that Eloy had been used as bait in a jaguar hunt and not seen again. A distraught Hadwin thanked him for the information, before grabbing his spear and heading into the rainforest.

Ixchel had heard the whole conversation and sprinted away ahead of Hadwin. She had already visited the camp so was able to find a quicker way of getting there. Her senses drew her back to Eloy's sleeping place where she sniffed the ground picking up his scent more strongly. From there she found the offal pit. Here his scent was harder to detect but she managed to catch enough of it to follow a trail and she quickly found the exposed jaguar pit. Peering over the edge, she saw Eloy lying crumpled at the bottom.

'Eloy,' she called, but there was no response. Unsure what to do, she sat on the edge, legs dangling over the side, contemplating her next move. A bird flew overhead, and she remembered the quetzal feather given to her in the city. She called out to it. 'Can you find Quie? Tell her Ixchel has need of her.'

In minutes the bird, Quie alighted on her shoulder.

'How can I help you, Ixchel the freer?'

She indicated the crumpled body at the base of the pit, 'My brother.'

The quetzal flew down, landing gently on Eloy's chest.

'Is he alive?' called Ixchel, although in her heart she knew that he was.

'I feel his heartbeat,' replied the bird flying back up, 'but in truth it is weak.'

'Can you get help to bring him up?'

Ixchel longed to jump down to her twin but that would only leave two of them trapped. Instead, she paced the perimeter. The forest appeared to be moving. Leaves were waving even though there was no breeze. She began to make out small figures and realised a horde of macaques were approaching, carrying leaves. Behind them a huge howler monkey was dragging a large branch which he carefully lowered into the pit, leaning it at an angle against the side. Once it was in position, he nimbly ran down and picked up Eloy, carrying him carefully to the surface and laying him at Ixchel's feet.

'Thank you, thank you,' she said. 'I owe you an enormous debt.'

'I am pleased to help you sister. I know that you are the freer.'

Before she could respond he had bounded off into the trees. While she examined Eloy, noting the head wound and the strange angle of his arm, the macaques, one by one, dropped their leaves into the pit, filling it up so that no other animals could be trapped in it.

'Thank you, thank you,' she said. 'May the blessings of Ek Balem fall on you.'

The monkeys acknowledged her thanks and ran away. Nitor, the kingsnake slithered into view.

Sister, what are you doing?' he asked, watching her test the success of the monkey's efforts.

'I'm testing this trap to make sure no other creature gets caught like my brother.'

'You always think of us rainforest animals. Unlike other humans.'

I prefer the rainforest and the animals,' she replied.

The snake watched her work.

'I cannot help with this task,' he said, 'Can I help in another way?'

Ixchel thought for a moment. 'Yes, she said, wiping her brow. 'Can you guide my father here to take my brother back to our village; he won't know the way? Will you make sure that he finds him?'

'I will see to it,' said Nitor.

'Thank you, brother,' said Ixchel, finishing her work. Satisfied that the pit had been sufficiently filled, she scampered away home. Nitor stealthily steered Hadwin. When he tried to go in the wrong direction, Nitor would appear and hiss at him so that he turned another way until he found Eloy.

Hadwin raced to his son, scooped him up and carried him as quickly as he could back to the village. It was further than he realised, and he had to stop several times to check his way. The journey was slow and it was dusk when he made it back home. Ixchel rushed to greet them. Spying the snake at the edge of the rainforest, she mouthed her thanks. He nodded and slithered back into the undergrowth.

Abha was waiting anxiously for news of her son and was greatly relieved to see them return.

'Quickly, in here,' she said. 'Ixchel, fetch the healer.'

Hadwin laid Eloy gently onto a pallet while Abha fetched warm water to clean the blood and offal off him, before transferring him to his bed. The healer arrived promptly and examined the boy.

'Sit him up Hadwin and hold him, his shoulder is out of place and I must push it back.'

Hadwin did as he was asked and there followed a sickening crack as the healer repositioned Eloy's shoulder. Afterwards, he tended to the bump on his head, administering a poultice to reduce the swelling. He also prepared a tincture of healing herbs for Abha to give him.

'He must take these every day until the new moon,' he said, handing her the bottle of liquid. 'Then, if the gods will it, he should recover.'

'Thank you,' said Abha. 'Thank you.'

The healer left and the three of them sat with Eloy, each saying their own silent prayers to Ahau-Chamahez, the god of healing, for his recovery. Hadwin also went to the priest to make an offering of food so that the god would be pleased and help their son. Night was drawing in when he returned, Abha sent him to rest and Ixchel too.

'I am his mother, I will watch him tonight,' she said, gently caressing Eloy's hand. 'You did your part, husband, in finding him. Go. Rest.'

Hadwin nodded, although it was many minutes before he reluctantly left his boy's side.

Ixchel wouldn't leave her brother, but Abha gently coaxed her, 'Sleep now daughter, you will need your strength for tomorrow so that you can keep vigil by him again.' She squeezed her hand softly and Ixchel reluctantly moved away, watching as Abha pulled a reed screen around her and Eloy, glad that her brother was being so well cared for. *Would they do the same for me?* she thought, in a moment of jealousy. But she knew that they would, despite how much she exasperated them. In the darkness of their little hut, she listened to her father's breathing get slower and settle into the steady rhythm of sleep. Abha too, began to tire and lay next to Eloy, holding tightly to his hand, before she also fell asleep.

Ixchel rose from her bed and tiptoed outside. The moon was behind clouds, the night was pitch black. Taking a few moments for her eyes to adjust, she strode away from the village before bounding into the rainforest. Deeper and deeper and faster and faster she ran, seeking out the place where she had met Ek Balem. Using only her instincts and sense of smell, she managed to weave her way to the location. Climbing a tree to avoid being vulnerable to an attack, she caught her breath and called out to the rainforest.

'Mighty Ek Balem, I wish to speak with you, if you would grant it.'

Unsure what to do next, she stretched herself, catlike, along the branch and waited. She lay back and watched a few wispy clouds scud across the night sky and a thousand stars stare back at her. To pass the time she tried to count them, but just when she thought she had them, they shifted and she had to start again. A low growl made her stop. Facing her on the opposite branch was a large black jaguar.

'You called, little one.'

'Yes, Lord Balem,' she replied, hurrying to sit up to talk to him properly.

'You have need of me?'

'Please, my brother Eloy. He is dying.'

Ek Balem snorted. 'He is not dying, merely sleeping. And even if he was dying, why should I save him? He has disappointed me with his desire to hunt for sport. I expected better from him.' Ek Balem flashed his claws as if contemplating a different fate for the boy. Ixchel flinched.

'Perhaps his time with the king will awake his true nature. Bring him to me at the next crescent moon after he awakes.' And then he was gone, leaving Ixchel half wondering if she had imagined the encounter.

She found her way back easily this time, no need of the kingsnake, reaching the hut in the early hours and crawling quietly to her bed, where sleep quickly embraced her. Her dreams were vivid; a jaguar roamed the village, lethal claws reaching for Eloy before moving on. The scene switched. This time twenty jaguars sat guard over her brother where he slept, letting no-one near until they parted to allow a sleek black jaguar to approach and breathe life into him. The cats melted away and he was surrounded by spears. A man in a tall headdress beckoned to a priest, who raised a sacrificial knife.

'Noooooooooo!' screamed Ixchel, sitting up in bed drenched in sweat. Throwing back her cover she dashed across to the screen. Her mother and brother were sleeping peacefully, her shout had not woken them. She knelt and took his hand, 'Brother, I will not let them harm you,' she whispered.

Abha stirred, smiling at her daughter. 'He has slept peacefully,' she said to reassure Ixchel. 'I believe he will recover.'

'He will, mother,' said Ixchel. 'He is strong and Ek Balem wills it.'

'We cannot know the will of the gods, child; nevertheless, we will make another offering and hope that it will be so.'

Ixchel nodded, 'I will make breakfast, mother. You rest.'

Abha grabbed her hand, 'You are a good girl, Ixchel. Thank you.'

Chapter Nine

A Close Encounter

Eloy slept for two more days before waking confused and disorientated. The swelling on the back of his head had gone, although the area was still tender, and he winced as he turned his head on the pillow. However, it was his shoulder that gave him the most pain. He tried to push himself up with that arm and moaned loudly.

Ixchel's black eyes smiled at him and he saw the shadow of a large cat sitting behind her.

'Welcome back brother,' she said.

'What happened?' he asked, staring beyond her, looking for the cat.

'What are you looking at?' said Ixchel, turning to see behind her.

'I...I thought I saw, it doesn't matter. Tell me.'

Ixchel filled him in; where they had found him and what he was covered in. Slowly the memory came back to him of being used as bait for the jaguar hunt. When he told her what the king had done to him, she listened in horrified silence.

'The strange thing is Ixchel, no cats came near. Not one and that really angered the king.'

She feigned astonishment at this, not wanting to reveal that she had sent out a warning.

'It is a good thing though,' he said, 'or I would have been torn to pieces. Although I would have liked to have seen one.' He shifted position and winced again.

'My shoulder?' he said.

'It was displaced,' she replied. 'The healer says it will be many moons before it is back to its normal strength. No more bow and arrow for you for a while.'

'I won't be needing it.' he said. 'I've had enough of hunting.'

Abha came home from the fields and hearing voices, rushed to her son's side.

'Eloy, Eloy, thank the gods,' she said, squeezing his hand. 'Ixchel fetch him atole, he must be ravenous.'

Ixchel went to the pot of maize porridge sitting in the fire embers to keep warm and put some into a bowl for her brother. In his weakened state he struggled to eat. With Abha coaxing him he gradually emptied the bowl, before drifting back to sleep.

Several times that day he woke, each time managing a small amount of food and drink to help renew his strength. It was a few more days before he felt well enough to get up, moving unsteadily at first and leaning on Hadwin for support. After that, his vigour and appetite returned quickly and Abha joked that he would empty their food store if he kept eating at the same rate. In reality, she was so thankful that he was alive, she would happily have let him.

At night, when it was just the two of them, Eloy would confide in Ixchel about the king's cruelty. How he hunted purely for sport and revelled in the bloodletting. How he had men beaten or sacrificed for no reason and how he had taken all the glory for himself when the two of them had gone hunting.

'That's why he left me to die,' he explained to her. 'He didn't want me telling anyone that I tracked and killed the deer, not him.'

'Did you want the glory?' she asked him.

'At first, yes. The day I returned to camp with a deer that I had single handedly killed, I felt so pleased with myself.' He dropped his eyes from her gaze. 'Ixchel, I was so arrogant. I thought only of myself, my skills, my prowess.' A tear fell as he continued. 'I forgot you sister and I forgot to respect the rainforest.'

Ixchel listened quietly, seeing the regret in his face.

'Eloy, I need to tell you something.' She took his hand. 'You know that I can communicate with the rainforest animals.' He nodded. 'Well, I warned the jaguars to stay away. I had no idea that the king would do that to you. I am so sorry, brother. Can you forgive me?'

Eloy was silent, mulling over this revelation. Ixchel waited anxiously.

'Sister, dear sister, you do not need forgiveness. If you hadn't warned them, I could have been eaten. Remember I was the bait.'

Ixchel squeezed him so hard he could barely breathe.

'Mind my shoulder,' he laughed, hugging her back.

'I can see in the dark too,' she told him, excitedly.

'You truly are blessed. I wish…I wish,' but he didn't finish because Abha came across to them. 'Sleep, children, it is late.'

They settled down and she kissed them both before retiring herself.

Each day, Eloy's physical strength returned. His shoulder took longer, but he exercised it every day to help it heal. His inner spark had been extinguished though. He no longer rose early to practise his hunting skills. His bow had to remain untouched because of his shoulder, but his spears, knives and traps were left too. Instead, he worked the land with Hadwin, refused to go on hunts for agouti unless forced and he shunned the company of the other boys. His parents observed the change; they said nothing, simply too relieved to worry about it.

When the night of the first crescent moon after Eloy's recovery arrived and she had to bring Eloy to Ek Balem, Ixchel lay worrying. Would he go with her, or would he try to stop her as he had done in the past? She feigned sleep until her parents were settled for the night. When the moon hung overhead, she felt the call, and gently woke Eloy, placing a hand over his mouth to prevent him from shouting out in surprise.

'Come with me brother. Quickly.'

Puzzled, he kicked off his blanket, pulled on his moccasins and followed her outside. Already she was disappearing into the rainforest and he had to run to catch up. Ixchel had no trouble finding the way, negotiating a path with ease. Eloy, who had always felt at home in the rainforest, marvelled at the way Ixchel moved so quietly, sometimes blending into her surroundings so well that he lost sight of her, and she had to retrace her steps to find him. Eventually, she stopped within a circle of chechen and chacah trees, which always grow together. Taking care not to touch the chechen trees, whose branches secreted a black poison that burnt skin, the twins sat down and waited.

'What are we doing here?' said Eloy.

'You'll see,' said Ixchel, then stiffened. 'He is here, stand up.'

Eloy, whose night vision was not as sharp as hers, could see nothing. Slowly, his eyes began to make out the shape of a large cat. Ixchel felt him grab her hand.

'Run!' he whispered.

'No. Be still,' she said.

The black jaguar approached, circling them both, before sitting down to face them.

'Thank you, Ixchel, for bringing your brother to me.'

Eloy looked from the cat to his sister astonished. 'Did it just talk to you? And how did I manage to understand?'

'It's Ek Balem,' whispered Ixchel. 'If he wants you to understand him, then you will.'

The jaguar turned his attention to Eloy.

'Do you know who I am, boy?'

Eloy, terrified, nodded.

'I am Ek Balem, god of the underworld, giver of life. I asked your sister to bring you here. Do you know why?'

He shook his head.

'Because you disappointed me with your wanton killing and your lack of humility.'

Eloy couldn't make eye contact, ashamed that the mighty god had seen his weakness and arrogance.

'I wish to speak to your brother alone, Ixchel. You may go. I will see that he is returned home.'

Ixchel bowed, smiled to Eloy and bounded off into the rainforest, free to roam as she pleased until dawn.

'Walk with me, boy,' commanded the jaguar god.

'I was there at your birth,' said Ek Balem. 'I watched and waited for your arrival. You were expected. The gods foresaw great things for you.'

He paused to examine a claw, letting his words sink in.

'Your sister, however, was a surprise.'

Eloy listened silently, trying to find the courage to voice the question he wanted to ask. Ek Balem looked at him.

'W…what things?'

'You have a destiny to fulfil. Do you know the prophecy?'

Eloy stared blankly at him.

'I thought not. It states: he who walks with jaguars shall know true greatness. True greatness boy, and your foolish bravado in front of the king was not part of it. You could have been killed. If your sister had not warned the jaguars of the king's intentions, you would be dead by now.'

'Ixchel, I know,' he spluttered.

'Your sister is…special,' said Ek Balem. 'She is one of us,' he said, indicating with his paw to the circle of jaguars that now surrounded them both. Eloy gasped at their beauty. The mottled yellow-brown fur perfectly camouflaging them so that he had been unaware of their approach.

'Have you brought me here to kill me?'

Ek Balem laughed, 'Your sister asked me the same thing the first time we met here. No boy, I have brought you here for you to see what it truly means to be amongst jaguars.'

He sat, as one by one, the big cats approached Eloy, sniffing him, circling him and walking on.

'We are not trophies for our pelts to be worn by men. To be hunted for no reason except false glory.' There was anger and pain in his words that struck home to Eloy as he remembered the king adorned in jaguar skins and still wanting more.

'Too many men hunt us for sport,' continued Ek Balem. 'You must stop them.'

'Me!' said Eloy. 'How can I?'

'You have walked amongst us now. You must find a way.'

The other cats had left, and Eloy was surprised to find that they were back at the outskirts of the village.

'Be who you were born to be,' said Ek Balem. 'It is nearly time.'

'Who is that?' asked Eloy, but he was alone. Puzzled, he meandered back home, creeping in unnoticed. There was no sign of Ixchel. He lay down, pulling his blanket over him and contemplated the night's events. What did it all mean? Who was he meant to be? And where was Ixchel? He really needed to talk to her. Round and round the questions went until he fell into an exhausted sleep.

Chapter Ten

Revelations

The next morning Eloy awoke to see Ixchel sleeping beside him. He pinched her arm to wake her. Stretching lazily, she smiled at him.

'Did your meeting go well? What did he say?'

Eloy moved his head in their parent's direction and put a finger to his lips. The two of them rose quietly and left the hut to find somewhere private to talk. They chose a spot at the edge of the village where the large palm fronds grew and sheltered them from view. The early morning dew sat on the leaves and they tipped some into their mouths and splashed their faces to wake up.

That's better,' said Ixchel, 'now tell me what did Lord Balem say?'

'He talked about a prophecy and that my birth was expected, and he said that I have to stop the king from hunting jaguars, and I am meant for great things.'

'Did he say anything about me?'

'He said that you were a mystery, but we know that,' he smiled. 'Ixchel, it is all so confusing. What great things could I possibly do? I am not even a hunter anymore, only a farmer.'

'You are far more than that,' she said. 'You have always been the strongest and fastest in our village and the most courageous.'

'Maybe once, but now I feel so…so empty.' To lighten his mood he said, 'Tell me, what did you do all night?'

Ixchel broke into a broad smile. 'I went deeper into the rainforest where the jaguar families meet. They are usually quite solitary creatures but on crescent moons they meet at a special glade to exchange news. Last night there weren't as many, but the mothers brought their cubs and we played together. Eloy, I felt so at home there. I can't put into words the joy I feel in their company.'

'The others came to see me,' said Eloy.

Ixchel jumped up at this news. 'They came to you. That's wonderful. What happened?'

He told her how they had all approached him. 'It felt like they were testing me somehow.'

'Well they didn't harm you, so you must have passed,' she grinned.

'But I didn't. He said I had disappointed him. What does it all mean? What did they want? I can't talk to them like you can.'

The sound of approaching footsteps ended their conversation. Some of the villagers had come to cut palm leaves for the roof of the village chief's hut that needed mending. The twins stayed to help, carrying armfuls of palm fronds back to the village, leaving them outside the chief's dwelling. Soon a large group of villagers began the task of weaving the palm fronds together and then a few of the men climbed up on to the roof and began laying out a new one. The happy buzz of activity distracted Eloy from his thoughts, and he was glad of it. When the children had done all they could, they went home where Abha was waiting anxiously for them.

'Where were you? Your father has already gone to the fields.'

'We were helping with the chief's hut, they were mending the roof,' said Ixchel.

'I am glad that you are joining in with the obligations of the village,' said Abha, 'but now you must eat quickly and get out to the fields.'

They grabbed bowls of atole, shovelling it down fast as their appetites kicked in. Even Ixchel ate well that morning. When they reached the fields, Eloy went to join Hadwin and the menfolk, whilst Ixchel and Abha worked with the women harvesting beans. Abha joined in with the gossip but Ixchel was too distracted with Eloy's account of the previous night to take much notice. When the day's work was done they headed home to prepare the evening meal. Hadwin and Eloy ate together inside so Ixchel had no chance to talk to him that evening, and by the time she and Abha had cleaned up the pots and prepared the atole for the morning Eloy was fast asleep.

The next few days settled into a similar pattern of hard work and early nights, giving Ixchel little chance to sit and talk with Eloy, who seemed distant and distracted. One evening, about a week after their conversation, she asked to go to the forest on the pretext of picking papaya.

'You can go but be back before sunset,' said Abha.

'I will mother, I promise,' she said and sprinted away, feeling her heart lift immediately she was free of the confines of village life. Making sure to at least pick a few papayas which she nestled at the base of a ceiba tree, she wandered happily through the greenery, listening to the mockingbirds or the screeching of the bright green parrots as they flew from tree to tree. Something rustled in the fallen leaves at the base of a zapote tree and her friend Silas the porcupine shuffled out.

'Well met, sister,' he said. 'Well met.'

Ixchel clapped her hands delightedly and sat down beside him.

'How is your brother? Is he recovered?'

'He is better,' said Ixchel. 'How did you know?'

'We witnessed the king's hunt. We have not seen him since you rescued him. He rarely comes into the rainforest.'

'He doesn't hunt anymore unless the village is desperate for food, then he will accompany father if he is forced to.' She sighed, touching her heart. 'The spark has gone from him. It's like he doesn't know how to be happy anymore.'

'He will be restored. Ek Balem will see to it.'

Ixchel shook her head. 'Ek Balem talked to him. That's made him worse.'

Silas turned to go, 'It is not yet his season. His time is coming.'

'Wait. What does that mean? Come back.'

But he had already gone, leaving her alone with yet more questions. Sighing, she gathered up her papayas and headed home hoping to have a conversation with Eloy. She found him sat outside the hut cleaning Hadwin's tools. She smiled encouragingly at him, but he remained distant, locked in by his self-doubt.

'Please talk to me Eloy. Let me help you,' she said.

'What can you do. I am the disappointment and I am the one supposed to stop the king,' he snapped. 'Why don't you run back to the forest and talk to your animal friends and leave me alone,' he said bitterly.

'Eloy, please. Don't be mean. Maybe I can talk to the jaguars for you.'

'And ask them what? How a failure can ever protect them from the men who hunt them?'

'We are still young. You will find a way.'

'We are twelve. I am almost a man. I used to hope that I would be a hunter warrior in the king's army and live in the city, but I want nothing to do with him. I hate him.'

There was such anger in his face that Ixchel recoiled. 'I've never seen you like this,' she muttered, walking disconsolately away.

Chapter Eleven

The King's Offering

King Cadmael sat on his throne, two-thirds of the way up the great pyramid. The failure of the hunt to kill a single jaguar still enraged him.

'How am I to display my prowess in battle if I do not have fresh jaguar skins to prove what a powerful fighter I am?'

His priests, standing either side of the throne, tried to placate him.

'But mighty Ahaw, you already have so many fine skins,' said one.

'Yes Sire, the people admire and fear you, such is your renown,' said the other.

'Do you think so?' said King Cadmael.

'Most definitely,' said both priests together.

'Then you are fools!' bellowed the king, standing up. 'Look at them,' said King Cadmael pointing to the bustling city below. 'Look at them. Going about their business. Do any of them stop to look up at me? Do they? No, they don't.'

The priests shuffled nervously. The king continued his rant.

'Scribes,' he called.

Two men approached the throne. They wore bright blue loin cloths and, on their heads, wore blue and red headdresses. At their necks hung heavy jade necklaces, all these adornments chosen to show off their wealth and status. Each carried sheafs of bark paper to write down the king's decrees.

'Majesty, what would you have us record for you?' they said in unison, while bowing low.

King Cadmael seated himself on the throne. 'You will write down that on this day, the majestic King Cadmael, prepared himself for a magnificent sacrifice to the great god Itzamna to show his glory and to bring wealth to our city.'

The scribes hurriedly wrote down his words while the priests looked on.

'And make sure to say that I demonstrated courage far beyond that of my predecessor.'

'Yes, Ahaw.'

'He was weak, whereas I am strong, which my actions today will demonstrate to all those ants down there,' he said contemptuously, indicating the city. 'You must say that huge crowds came to the pyramid to observe my sacrifice and share in the glory.'

He turned to the priests, 'Summon my warriors. Call the people. They must bear witness to my bloodletting for the gods, and gasp at my bravery.'

He stormed off to the temple at the top of the pyramid, taking the steps two at a time. Another priest waited at the top. The two below hurriedly sent out messengers, telling the warriors to gather at the foot of the pyramid and bring their households with them. Street sellers and artisans were also summoned. By noon, the central courtyard and Pok-a-tok arena were filled with people. Satisfied with the size of the crowd, the two priests ascended the pyramid steps from the throne to the temple, carrying King Cadmael's ceremonial robes and new headdress, an elaborate affair of woven quetzal feathers, a stretched jaguar skin and a brightly coloured mask depicting a two-headed serpent. They entered the temple and dressed the king, whose mood had lifted a little, hearing the crowd below calling his name.

'They are about to bear witness to my greatness once again,' he said.

When he was ready in full ceremonial dress, he strode out of the temple to the cheers of the waiting crowd. He stood, arms folded, allowing the crowd's adulation to wash over him.

'People, my people,' he said, holding his arms open to them. 'You have come here today to witness the greatness of your ruler as I sacrifice my blood to the gods to bring honour and glory to our city.'

More cheers rose up on the breeze.

'Observe my power as I offer up my blood.'

He then pulled a sacrificial knife from his belt. The handle was made of jade, intricately carved with the face of the deity K'inich Ahau the sun god. The blade was a large piece of jagged edged obsidian, tapering to a sharp point. One of the priests stepped forward. The king knelt on one knee to allow the priest to remove the enormous headdress, which he placed with great reverence at the king's side. A second priest stepped forward holding out a sheet of amate, a special paper made from tree bark. This he placed on the king's left shoulder. King Cadmael held the knife aloft and then proceeded to cut his left ear. The blood ran down, collecting on the amate. He made a second incision, then a third, all to uproarious cheers from the onlookers below. Cadmael barely winced at the pain, determined to show his citizens how courageous their ruler was.

Once the bark was soaked in blood, the priest at his left stood up and retreated inside the temple. The priest on the king's right, replaced the headdress, taking care not to further damage the king's bloodied ear.

King Cadmael stood tall, 'My people, today you have seen power and strength. You know that the gods will be pleased with my offering. Return to your mundane lives secure in the knowledge that your city is watched over by such a wondrous leader.'

He strode towards the temple. At the entrance his headdress was removed once more. He went in to find the third priest preparing a small fire. When the blaze was ready, priest number two, handed King Cadmael the blood soaked amate for him to place in the fire, completing the ritual; the burning symbolising the transfer of the offering to the gods via the rising smoke.

The ceremony finished, King Cadmael retired to his chambers where his ceremonial robes and headdress were put away and his wounds tended. Buoyed up by the success of his offering, he called his two captains to him.

'Today you saw the courage of your ruler,' he said to them, striding across his chamber. 'The gods are pleased with my efforts, now it is your turn to please me.'

The captains waited for him to continue.

'We will conquer our neighbours; seize their lands, and take slaves to expand our city.'

A roar of approval from the captains echoed around the room.

'Gather your best warriors. We will attack at the new moon.'

And so began a brutal series of raids on the two city states closest to Yaxchilan. King Cadmael ordered his troops to show no mercy; to take prisoners and sacrifice them to the gods to display his greatness. Some were brought back to

Yaxchilan to play Pok-a-tok for the crowds and to allow King Cadmael to show off his triumphs to his citizens. He sat on his throne clothed in his best jaguar pelts and wearing the most extraordinary headdresses topped with brightly coloured metre-long feathers to watch these matches. During this time, the people of Yaxchilan held festivals and made extra offerings to the gods to thank them for the successes in war, and they heaped praises upon their king. These conquests brought great wealth to the king, the captains, warriors and priests and Cadmael's reputation as a king to be feared, spread far and wide. Weapon-makers prospered too, their workshops constantly busy replenishing the army's stock of spears, knives, bows and arrows.

Although many people in the upper echelons benefitted from the wars, the lower ranks of society suffered. The merchants lost out on their regular trade with their neighbours. The farmers struggled; their crops were commandeered to feed the army. The populace started out enjoying the victory celebrations, but they soon grew weary of them. Wars were costly in money and lives. Too many young men were sent to fight and even though Cadmael's armies were successful, many were killed or injured. As the wars raged on, the citizens of Yaxchilan longed to revert to the days of peaceful trade with their neighbours but the king basked in the glory of his conquests and continued to beat the drums of war.

Chapter Twelve

Celebrations

In the village, Eloy and Ixchel worked long hours tending the fields with the rest of their community. Soldiers came every few days and took sacks of grain, papaya, potatoes, beans and any other available crops. Many times the villagers were left short of food, but they knew better than to complain.

Ixchel escaped to the rainforest at every crescent moon. It was the only thing that kept her spirits up. Each time the pull of the rainforest grew stronger and took her further and further into its heart. She always ended up at the jaguar enclave where she was welcomed as one of their own. They showed her their secret paths and taught her how to hunt like a cat.

'You have our instincts,' remarked one of the jaguars one evening. 'I have never seen a human with your talents.'

'Ek Balem gave me them, but I don't know why. I do know that being here with you all is where I feel the most understood.' She played with the cubs, rolling on her back while they practised their pouncing on her. A cub jumped playfully on her shoulder and she held him aloft, the sound of her laughter ringing through the trees.

'I don't fit with the people. I'm always getting things wrong and annoying them,' she said, when the cubs had run off. 'And I wish Eloy would come with me when I visit you. You would let him, wouldn't you?'

The jaguars remained silent for a while, then Udyr, the senior cat spoke, 'We would not attack him but he has yet to earn his place among us as you have.'

'But how can he do that?'

'His path will become clearer. Be patient, young one.'

Ixchel sighed, 'I miss him; we don't talk about things anymore. He avoids me all the time and I don't know why.' A tear fell as she said this.

******

On one of these visits, she found a small cenote and as it was an unusually hot night, she decided to swim. The cubs paced the water's edge, unsure whether to join her. Ixchel swam with smooth easy strokes, enjoying the coolness of the water on her skin.

'Come on in,' she called to the cubs, beckoning to them to join her. Tentatively, they put their paws into the water, then plunged right in, swimming like they were born to it. Other jaguars appeared, swimming with them to cool off, sometimes seizing the black fish for a quick snack. Looking around her, Ixchel wondered when she had last felt this carefree. Village life was becoming increasingly stifling and she wasn't sure how much longer she could endure it. She knew that her parents would soon be casting around for a suitable husband. More than ever, she was glad of her fragile start in life; her rounded forehead and wild reputation made her much less appealing to potential suitors than the other girls with the traditional flat foreheads. She waded ashore and glanced at her reflection while these thoughts raced around her mind. The moonlight didn't show her face, only a jaguar's. Puzzled, she looked behind to see who stood at her shoulder. No-one was there. Her hands flew to her face, but only the soft touch of skin met her fingers, no fur or whiskers. *Trick of the light,* she thought moving away from the water.

The cubs went to their mother who had returned from hunting and Ixchel wended her way back to the settlement.

Eloy watched his sister sneak in at dawn envying her her night of freedom. These days his heart was always heavy, weary and he didn't know why. Each day was filled with toil, tending fields, harvesting crops, mending tools. Usually he enjoyed this work, taking satisfaction in a job well done, or enjoying the fruits of their labour at mealtimes. But the wars on the neighbouring cities had been going on for months and there was a sombre mood among his people. The constant drain on their supplies by the king's armies left many families hungry. That melancholy hung over him like a storm cloud, reaching inside to squeeze his heart.

'Ixchel,' he whispered, 'lend me your free spirit. I have dire need of it.'

She crept close to him. 'What troubles you, dear brother,' she asked tenderly.

'Ixchel, I feel as if all the cares of the village rest on my shoulders.'

She saw the tears welling in his eyes as he spoke. Taking both of his hands in hers, she pulled him closer, 'This is Ek Balem's doing. He has marked you in some way.'

Eloy sighed, 'I wish he had given me more answers. Nothing he said makes sense. He has such high expectations of me. How can I ever meet them?'

'Brother, you will find a way. Things will become clearer.'

Their parents stirred, pausing their conversation. Hugging each other tightly, they readied themselves for the day ahead. Eloy felt a little stronger that morning, his spirits lifted a little. No soldiers came for food supplies for a week, so the villagers allowed themselves to eat well. Cadmael's men had raided the stores of their latest conquest, leaving the people of Yaxchilan to enjoy their own crops for once.

King Cadmael now ruled three city states and tributes poured in, filling his coffers with treasure and his grain stores with food. He had commissioned an enormous statue of himself to be erected in the centre of Yaxchilan in honour of his victories. When it was ready, he declared a feast day to celebrate. Eloy felt the villager's excitement like a fizz of electricity in his soul. After so many months of hardship, the chance to party came as an immense relief. Even Ixchel caught the mood and allowed herself to share in her parent's joy. In a rare act of generosity, King Cadmael, having been persuaded by one of his priests that it would please the gods, sent messengers to distribute food to the villages to celebrate the statue's unveiling. The priest had in fact been informed by his spies that there was growing discontent, particularly amongst the farmers about the cost of the wars. He suggested to Cadmael that the citizens would worship their king still further if they felt rewarded for their support and, of course, it would be a wonderful way for him to demonstrate his greatness. The flattery worked and the citizens of Yaxchilan cheered his name loudly during the festivities.

The farmers from several settlements gathered on the outside of the city walls to cook and share in the celebration. The women prepared food together. All the children under fourteen were allowed to play. They ran races, played with wooden toys, had games of hide and seek or sat together sharing stories. Eloy and Ixchel, taking care not to be followed by any of the little ones, snuck away and back home to their secret cenote. Down the tunnel they went, barefooted now, moccasins having been discarded at the entrance. Eloy faltered when the light diminished, and he struggled to see clearly. Not Ixchel, her night vision was as sharp as the day. She ran on ahead laughing and Eloy heard the splash of her jumping into the cool water. It took him a little longer to catch up.

'How did you do that?' he asked.

'Do what?' said Ixchel.

'Get down the path so easily. I couldn't see a thing.'

She shrugged, 'I told you, remember, that I can see in the dark. Anyway, it's only dark for a short way, isn't it?'

Sunlight flooded the centre of the pool through the hole in the roof, lighting up their happy faces.

'See that patch of moss on the wall over there,' said Ixchel pointing to a splodge of red. Eloy nodded.

'Race you.' and she was off, legs kicking furiously. Eloy went after her, his long smooth strokes making easy work of the distance. He reached the edge just ahead of her, turning to see her grinning broadly. 'Back,' she yelled, somersaulting under water before kicking off from the wall. This time she was too quick. Back and forth they raced, or dived for fish, or jumped in from a rocky outcrop high up on one of the walls. Sometimes they simply floated lazily under a sunbeam to catch their breath before racing again, until they collapsed exhausted and laughing on the shore. Ixchel nestled into Eloy's shoulder; his arms wrapped around her. Neither spoke; the distance of the last few months was finally erased, and the closeness of their bond restored. It was only the rumbling of their tummies that drew them back to the feast. Eloy's stomach grumbled so loudly it echoed around the cenote producing peals of laughter from Ixchel, whose own stomach then did the same. Giggling helplessly, they staggered to their feet. Ixchel caught Eloy's hand, guiding him through the dark. They found their moccasins and emerged from the tunnel hand in hand and wandered back to the villagers.

The feast was underway when they got back. Huge cooking pots filled with steaming hot bean stew sat on smouldering embers in large fire pits dug out for the occasion. The twins ran up, grabbed a bowl each, filled them with stew and took a hunk of maize bread from a table stacked up with it and sat and ate heartily. They were on their third bowlful when their mother found them.

'Here you are,' said Abha, 'we missed you.'

'We went swimming,' said Eloy.

'That is good for your shoulder,' said Abha. 'Come and join us. Your father and I have news.' She cast a knowing look in Ixchel's direction when she said this, leaving Ixchel with a sinking feeling in the pit of her stomach that had nothing to do with the amount of beans she had eaten.

Abha led them back to where Hadwin was sat with another family, a man and woman and two small girls.

'Ixchel, this is Fabio and his wife Cualli, they have been waiting to meet you,' said Hadwin.

The couple stood and greeted her. She felt their scrutiny as they studied her face and limbs.

'Her forehead is round,' said Abha, 'because she was such a weak baby, we didn't think that she would live more than two moons; but the gods were kind to us and she has grown strong.'

'That will not worry our son,' said Fabio.

To illustrate his point, a young man of about fifteen years approached the group. Hadwin

128

watched him, *he looks fit and strong,* he thought. The boy grimaced at his parents and sat watching his younger sisters playing their game of stones. He waited until they had carefully built a tower of stones, then, when they were trying to get their mother to see their skill, he deliberately kicked the tower over, laughing at their upset faces. Then he picked up the stones, aiming them at birds perching in the trees or at a group of young boys playing races, smiling when he hit one.

Abha watched him commit these acts. Noticing the worried look on Abha's face Cualli said, 'Kan is a fine farmer. Fabio has taught him. He knows how to plant and tend crops. Your daughter will not go hungry.' Then to hide her anxiety she added, 'No-one else will marry your daughter with her strange looks and wild ways.'

'Marry me!' blurted out Ixchel. 'Mother, I have no wish to marry.'

'Whether you wish it or not, it is the way of things,' said Hadwin crossly. He turned to Fabio, 'If your son can grow crops and build a house then the match can go ahead. The betrothal ceremony will be in three moons when she is thirteen and then they can marry when she turns fourteen.'

Satisfied with this outcome, Fabio and Cualli and their three children left to rejoin their own villagers. Once they were out of earshot Ixchel pleaded with her parents.

'Please, please don't make me marry him.'

Abha raised her hand, 'Ixchel we have approached every family with a son of marriageable age. All have refused.'

'Good,' said Ixchel.

'It is not good,' said Abha. 'A girl must marry. Kan is the only boy who will agree.'

'Please no. Not him. Not anyone.'

'Enough!' shouted Hadwin. 'We have agreed and that is an end to it.'

'I hate you!' shouted Ixchel and ran off. Eloy made to go after her.

'Leave her,' said Hadwin. 'Today is a feast day and even if she is not celebrating this news, we are.'

Reluctantly, Eloy stayed and joined in the celebrations. When Hadwin left to talk to a group of farmers Eloy spoke to Abha, 'Does she have to be married? Can't she stay with us?'

'Eloy, it is the way of things. We will be finding you a bride soon, but we had to secure a place for your sister first.'

'But you saw how unhappy she was.'

'It is the way of things,' said Abha. 'She will come round.'

Eloy shook his head, made an excuse and wandered home to try to find his sister.

Ixchel ran and ran. There was only one place to go. She had to find Ek Balem. *This can't happen,* she thought. *I can't marry. I can't live a confined life.* She didn't stop until she reached the grove of trees at their usual meeting place. To her surprise, Ek Balem was waiting for her.

'They are making me get married,' she blurted out. 'What am I to do? I hate them.'

Ek Balem said nothing, merely sat patiently while she calmed down, letting her anger and fear dissipate. Several other jaguars arrived and formed a semi-circle around her.

'Child,' said Ek Balem. 'Do not blame your parents. They are doing what they believe to be best for you. Accept what they say without fear. All will be well.' He walked away. 'Return home until the crescent moon, then come amongst us as usual.'

One by one the big cats came up to her and rubbed their cheeks against hers in a gesture of friendship, before they too, set off for the night's hunting. Miserably, Ixchel made her way home and curled up on her sleeping mat, closing her eyes to blot out the unexpected turn the day had taken. By the time Eloy got back, she was fast asleep.

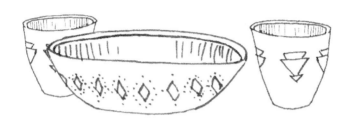

Chapter Thirteen

Visitors and Gossip

The next morning Eloy was whisked away early by Hadwin to set traps for agouti so he had no time to talk to his sister. Abha bustled about waiting for Ixchel to rise. When she did, she was withdrawn and sullen.

'Child, it is no good sulking. It is our duty as parents to find you a husband.'

'Even if I don't want one,' snapped Ixchel.

'It doesn't matter what you want. A girl must marry. You know that.'

'But why? Why can't I decide for myself?'

'Because that is not the way things are done. You should be grateful that we have managed to secure you a match. It was not easy.'

'I wish you hadn't.'

Abha sighed and left the hut. 'Time for work, there is nothing more to say.'

Ixchel joined her mother in the maize fields, working in solitary silence to clear the weeds. The other girls rarely approached her anyway so no-one saw her tears falling. Even Abha kept a distance. In her heart she felt guilty about the match they had made, but girls had to be married so what else was she to do?

It was late in the afternoon when the sound of girlish laughter caused Ixchel to look up from her weeding. To her horror, she could see Cualli and Kan heading in her direction. Cualli was waving. The other girls looked to see who they were waving at. Some of them admired Kan's fine physique and he returned their admiring glances.

'For you.' said Kan churlishly, holding out a tunic and a set of wooden beads.

'The first of Ixchel's dowry items,' said Cualli.

'Dowry,' whispered the girls. 'Did you hear that? The wild one is getting married.'

'Thank you,' said Ixchel, sensing the other girls' delight at her discomfort and taking the proffered gifts. She heard their whispers.

'That boy's too old for her,' said one.

'I heard that he was the only one they could find for her,' said another.

'I feel sorry for him,' said a third, which resulted in more laughter.

Ixchel wanted so badly to react to their jibes. Handing the gifts to her mother she led their visitors away from the fields with clenched fists. Through gritted teeth she offered them food and drink while the mothers talked. She sat silently. Kan paced around kicking dirt at the line of clean clothes draped over the low fence outside their home.

'Don't do that,' said Ixchel, 'you will dirty them.'

He stared at her and then kicked the dirt more vigorously, before striding over, lifting the garments and trampling them into the ground.

'You can wash them again.'

When Ixchel bent to pick them up, he took her hand and squeezed it tightly, digging his nails into her flesh, watching her closely, daring her to cry out.

'Don't ever tell me what to do,' he snarled.

Ixchel glared back at him but did not react.

Abha called to them, and he dropped her hand. The two sat with their mothers, Ixchel placing as much distance as she could between her and Kan.

When the food and drink were finished, Cualli stood up to leave. Ixchel rose too. Cualli took her hands and said, 'We are proud to welcome you to our family.'

Ixchel merely nodded a response.

'Come on Kan, we must leave now.' The boy stood and strode off ahead of his mother.

'He is anxious to work,' said Cualli to hide her embarrassment at his rudeness.

Ixchel cleared the cups and bowls, leaving the tunic and beads on the ground where she had dropped them. Abha picked them up and was about to reprimand her daughter for her lack of care until she saw the sad look of resignation on Ixchel's face.

'You will come round to the marriage,' said Abha. 'And it is another year away and, in that time, I will make sure you have all the skills you need to be a good wife.'

'There will never be enough time for that,' said Ixchel.

Each day, Ixchel's unhappiness deepened. Eloy sat with her in the evenings, but she rarely spoke even to him. He felt the depths of her despair at the impending betrothal and tried to persuade their parents to postpone it, but Hadwin was adamant.

'She must be married,' he said.

Ixchel worked like an automaton. She never smiled and only spoke when absolutely necessary. At night she clung tightly to Eloy, seeking comfort in their sibling bond and fearing their separation. It wasn't until the first crescent moon after the announcement, that Eloy caught a glimpse of her old self as she prepared to sneak off.

'Can I come with you?' he asked.'

She shook her head, 'Best not to, in case…' she gestured towards Hadwin. 'No point both of us getting into trouble if I am caught,' she said. 'Don't worry, I am quite safe out there.'

Immediately she sensed the parents were asleep, she crept out and away. Eloy followed a few minutes later to watch her leave, but he only spied a glimpse of a large cat moving away which made him even more concerned for her safety.

Ixchel, bursting with a sense of freedom, raced through the rainforest until she reached the jaguar grounds. Her friends greeted her. The cubs, much larger now, pounced excitedly around her.

'Swimming,' they chorused.

Laughing, Ixchel led the way to the cenote. Pausing at the water's edge to take in her reflection, instead of her own miserable face, it was a jaguar looking back at her. *Wishful thinking,* she thought to herself as she pulled off her tunic and dived in. When she surfaced, she longed to see paws instead of hands and a tail stretching out behind her but she was still herself. She swam, dived, caught fish and played with the cubs until the first streaks of dawn appeared, feeling more at home than she had ever been. *How I long to stay like this. This is where I belong, not married to some mean boy, working the land and bearing children. I might just as well live in a cage for it is the same thing for me.* With a deep sigh, she climbed out of the water. Heart heavy, she picked up her tunic, said her goodbyes and headed for home before her presence was missed.

Chapter Fourteen

Desolation

On her walk back home Ixchel touched the trees, watched the birds stirring and listened to their songs. *I must fill my heart with you* she said to herself, *because once I am married, I won't be able to come back.* The rainforest listened, and the trees sighed for her. She was late back, and her parents were already up when she approached the hut.

'Is your headache better?' asked Abha, when she entered.

'I told mother that you woke with a bad head and went for a walk,' said Eloy.

Smiling gratefully at her twin, Ixchel said, 'Yes, a little, thank you.'

'Have breakfast,' said Abha, 'and stay at home this morning if you are unwell. Join me at midday.'

The offer was well meant, but Ixchel knew it stemmed from her mother's guilt at the impending betrothal.

When everyone had gone to their day's work, Ixchel wandered back to the edge of the rainforest and climbed a tree. From her vantage point she could see if anyone approached the hut. Although she had been given the morning off, she was supposed to be resting at home and wanted to be sure she had time to get back if anyone came to check on her. Her fingers stroked the bark, feeling all the lumps and bumps against her skin and breathing in the delicious woody scent. *This is heaven,* she thought, lying back along the branch soaking up the sun's warmth. Something brushed her leg and she looked down to see the kingsnake, Nitor, sidling up beside her.

'Welcome brother snake,' she said, unfazed by his proximity. Nitor slithered past her and settled in a dip just above her where three branches forked. He observed her for several minutes before he spoke.

140

'You are human, yet now you have the aura of a jaguar. How is that possible?'

'Maybe because I spend so much time with them,' said Ixchel.

'No,' said the snake, 'that is not the reason. There is something else. Something within you.'

Ixchel laughed, 'All that's within me is a love of the rainforest. It is where I feel most alive.'

'Perhaps,' said Nitor, 'but I don't think so. And you can speak with us. That is not the human way.'

'True,' said Ixchel, dreamily, 'but that is because of Ek Balem. Although, the ancient tales do tell of humans and animals communicating.'

'The old tales,' scoffed Nitor, 'you mean the ones that talked of jaguars ruling this land. Do you see that happening?'

'Well, no,' said Ixchel, 'but…but it would be better. Jaguars only hunt for what they need, and they don't destroy the rainforest the way humans do.'

'They don't start wars either,' said Nitor.

Ixchel thought of the long months of fighting that King Cadmael had engaged in.

'Greed. It's all about greed,' she said, sitting up and looking out at the rainforest.

'If I were queen, I would make everyone share. And I would be friends with the neighbouring cities not try to conquer them. And I would reward people for kindness,' she said, warming to her theme. 'And I would ban the killing of birds and animals just for their feathers or pelts.' She thought about her friend, Silas the Porcupine, 'And I would let everyone show their true colours without fear of capture, because putting animals in cages would be against the law.'

She looked at Nitor, who appeared to be laughing.

'A fine speech,' he said. 'As if a farmer's daughter like you could ever be queen.'

'Maybe I can't,' she said, 'but I could try to change the way people behave. Help them take better care of the rainforest. I shall start with my new family.'

She jumped down from the tree and bounced off to the fields.

She has a jaguar's heart, thought Nitor, watching her walk away, the shadow of a cat beside her.

Ixchel's positive frame of mind stayed with her on her way to the fields as she thought about how she would influence her new family and community to take better care of the rainforest and its animals. However, it soon evaporated when Abha greeted her.

'Tonight, we are going to eat with Kan's family at their village so that you can be introduced to the elders,' said Abha.

Seeing Ixchel's brow crumple, she added, 'It is to help you settle in. You won't be a stranger to them.'

'Please, do we have to? I don't mind waiting for the ceremony.'

'Child, it is only one moon away. It is better like this.'

At that moment, Ixchel could not see how anything could make the situation better, but she kept those thoughts to herself.

'You must wear the dress and beads that Cualli and Kan brought for you. I will braid your hair. Go and bathe in the cenote and then I will prepare you.'

Ixchel dutifully did as she was told, her spirits sinking with every step. Despite her earlier bravado about influencing her new people, the cold reality of her situation closed around her like the walls of a cell. Even the cooling waters of the pool couldn't wash away her cares and her fears for the future. She swam and swam her tears mixing with the waters of the cenote. All sense of time was lost, and she remained in the pool until Eloy ran down to the water's edge and called her.

'Ixchel, you have to come home now.'

Swimming as slowly as she could, she edged towards the shore. He could see that she had been crying and struggled to find the right thing to say.

'I will be with you tonight. Stay close to me. It will be all right.'

'How can it ever be right, Eloy? I am being betrothed to a boy I don't know and don't want to know.' She squeezed out the water from her hair, sighing heavily. 'And I won't be living here so you and I will never see each other.'

'We still have a year before you are to be married,' he said, trying not to reveal the dread that he too felt at their separation. She had always kept him steady when his spirits sagged, cheering him up with her tales of the jaguars. How could he do the same for her in this situation?

'We will fill the days with as many adventures as we can. You can take me to the jaguars and introduce me to your other animal friends. And I will cover for you when you need time in the forest.'

'I love you Eloy,' she said, 'but that isn't going to change my future.' She pulled on her moccasins. 'Come on, I may as well face it.' Shoulders hunched and head down she exited the cenote. Sensing that she didn't want to talk any more, he simply linked arms with her as they meandered back home.

Abha fussed around her daughter, combing her long black hair and plaiting it neatly. When Ixchel had donned the tunic and beads, Abha stood back to admire her.

'You look beautiful,' she said.

I may look it, but I don't feel it, thought Ixchel, smiling weakly at her mother. Abha bustled around gathering the food offerings she was taking and calling to Eloy and Hadwin to get ready. When Abha was finally happy with everything, they set off.

Cualli and Fabio welcomed them and took them to meet the elders. Some other villagers appeared, curious to see who Cualli had managed to convince to marry her bullying son. They were surprised to see such a strong girl but acknowledged to each other that she didn't fit the usual idea of beauty and wondered at the match. The priest performed a blessing on the young couple and then the two families shared a meal, finished off with a dark chocolate drink. Ixchel barely touched her food, even turning down the hot chocolate, which was usually her favourite.

'Pre ceremony nerves,' said Abha, when she saw Cualli looking at the unfinished plate. 'It is the same at home.'

Cualli half smiled and turned to her son, Kan, who had guzzled his meal and gone back for more, his appetite clearly unaffected.

The conversation drifted from crops to hunting, the dowry, the wars, everyone hoping the king would soon be satisfied with his conquests. The evening eventually drew to a close and Ixchel's family rose to go home. More gifts were exchanged before they left.

'Until the new moon,' said Cualli.

'Yes, the new moon,' said Abha.

Ixchel muttered her goodbyes, then followed her parents. She walked arm in arm with Eloy, fragile as a broken branch about to fall.

'The parents are nice people,' said Eloy, 'they will look after you. And I will make sure somehow that I can come and visit. 'It may not be as bad as you think.'

'No, it will be far worse,' said Ixchel. 'Far worse.'

Chapter Fifteen

An Unexpected Outcome

The days until the new moon passed far too quickly for Ixchel. Busy days in the fields with Abha or mending clothes and sewing new ones to wear at the ceremony only served to speed up time. Each night before bed, she would sit in the nearest tree staring despondently into the rainforest, unsure how she would cope without it. Hadwin wanted to stop her, but Abha persuaded him to let her have this indulgence in a bid to raise her spirits. Eloy often sat with her, balancing on another branch. He too, was a good climber, but he lacked her innate sense of balance in the trees.

'Tomorrow is the last crescent moon before my betrothal,' she said.

'I know,' he replied, 'don't you think I am counting the days too?' He looked across at Ixchel, her pinched face, and thin arms.

'You should eat more,' he said. 'Kan's family will expect you to work hard.'

Ixchel laughed.

'What's funny?'

'I was thinking what a pair we will make, the wild girl and the mean boy. Two misfits palmed off on each other.'

'At least he won't be expecting conversation, only obedience,' said Eloy.

'When have I ever done as I was told?' laughed Ixchel.

Abha listened to the laughter and hoped her daughter was finally accepting her future.

Shortly before midnight they climbed down from their perch and crept inside to sleep, all sense of their earlier cheerfulness long gone, a shroud of despair had once more settled itself over Ixchel.

The next day was Eloy's thirteenth birthday, with Ixchel being born in the hour after midnight, they celebrated hers the following day. Hadwin and Abha took him to the village priest for a blessing before the day's work began. For Ixchel it dragged on and on, her mind firmly focused on the night to come. Her impending birthday heralded only a betrothal that she dreaded.

When night fell, she raced away to the rainforest without even waiting for her parents to sleep. With it being so close to the ceremony, they were less strict than usual so she knew they wouldn't be checking on her. *Eloy will cover for me anyway,* she thought.

She let her fingers brush every tree she passed, wanting to imprint the memory of their bark into her mind. The air smelled sweeter for her tonight and the stars shone brighter. As she approached the jaguar's meeting place in the glade of chechen and chacah trees she could feel the air bristling with his magic and knew that this space was protected by the jaguar god so that only those that belonged could find it. He was waiting for her.

'Ek Balem,' she said, bowing her head.

'Come and sit with me, child. It is nearly midnight, and we can mark your birthday together.'

150

She followed him through the trees until he stopped at a small cenote. This one was shallow with a wide opening in the roof, flooding it with moonlight. The two of them sat silently on the shore letting the hour tick by.

'I am to be betrothed in three days,' said Ixchel miserably, breaking the silence.

'I don't think so child,' said Ek Balem. 'Your life is going to take a new direction.'

'How can it?' she replied. 'Everything is mapped out for me. Husband, house, babies.'

'Is that what you think?' said Lord Balem.

'It's what I know,' she replied.

'We cannot definitely know our futures. Things change.'

'Not for the girls in our villages. We all know what our lives will be.'

'If you could choose, what life would you have?'

'That's easy,' she replied. 'I would live in the rainforest amongst the animals and I would take care of the plants and repair the damage that people do.' She was in full flow now. 'And I would bring Eloy to meet the jaguars and tell him to talk to the people to leave the forest in peace.'

'Would you not want him to live in the forest with you?'

'I would and he does love the rainforest, but he is drawn to the city. He is not satisfied being a farmer.'

'To live amongst the jaguars you must be one,' said Ek Balem.

'Nitor, the kingsnake, said I had the aura of a jaguar, Does that count?' said Ixchel.

'You have more than that,' said Ek Balem. 'Look,' he said, indicating the water.

Ixchel leaned forward to take in her reflection. What she saw amazed her. There was no girl anymore, only jaguar. She sprang up, then looked again and again. Could this be true or was it some cruel trick of the night?

'You are mine now,' said Ek Balem. 'I gave you life thirteen years ago and now I have called you back to me. This is your life now, to live free amongst the jaguars as one of us. There will be no wedding.'

Ixchel danced with happiness. To live in her beloved rainforest, to be a jaguar. She ran back to the water to look again, held up her paws examining every part of them, turning round and round to chase her tail before letting out a roar of joy. Everything made sense now. The capacity to communicate with animals, the aura, her ability to climb trees and hunt without being seen.

'When I breathed life into you, I gave you the heart and soul of a jaguar, but I let you stay with your brother as long as I could.'

'Thank you, thank you,' said Ixchel, bouncing around. 'Eloy. Eloy. I must tell him.'

'No.' said Ek Balem. 'If you return to your village tonight you will have to remain human.'

'But…'

'I will send word that you are safe and he is not to look for you.'

Ek Balem placed a giant paw on her shoulder. 'That path is closed to you now. From tonight, all humans are your enemy. If they see you, they will hunt you ceaselessly for your pelt.'

'They hunt all of us for our pelts,' said Ixchel, 'Why am I so special?'

'Because I have made you in my image.' said Ek Balem.

This time Ixchel studied her reflection more carefully.

'Oh…oh,' she said.

'Yes,' said Ek Balem. 'You are a black jaguar like me. The rarest and most sought after. Only the deepest rainforest is safe for you now.'

'But you visit the humans,' she said.

'I am a god. I can choose to be visible or not. Whilst you are well camouflaged, the best hunters could still track you.' he stared gravely into her eyes. 'And if they knew of your existence, trust me, they would come.'

'But Eloy is my twin. He would not hunt me.'

'Eloy is human and therefore a danger. He must have no knowledge of you.'

Ixchel felt the tears falling.

'This is the only way, little one.'

'How can I spend my life without him?'

'I will see to it that your human memories fade. Once you have lived amongst for a while you will forget that you were ever one of them and you will stop missing him.' He waited, letting all of this sink in.

Ixchel couldn't imagine ever forgetting her beloved twin, but to be a jaguar and live free in the rainforest was more than she had ever dared to hope for.

'Well. Are you staying?'

'Yes, yes,' said Ixchel, rejoicing in her new form, stretching, jumping, swishing her tail, flashing her claws. The other jaguars came to greet her, roaring their welcome to the family. They took her deeper and deeper into the forest. The distance didn't worry her. She moved with speed and grace, quickly overtaking the others. How glorious to run like this. When they needed to rest, they climbed trees, filling the branches like a flock of exotic birds.

Once rested, they padded on silent paws through the undergrowth. Ixchel could hear the sound of running water. The ground became muddier, and the air smelt fresher. They edged through the leaves and before her was a large pool fed by a waterfall that cascaded loudly over the rocks. She crouched down, sniffing the air for any scent of danger; then, with the other jaguars watching on, she sprang high into the air, stretching out her body and landing joyfully in the centre of the pool. For the first time in her life, she felt truly free and at one with the world.

Part Two

Chapter Sixteen

Ixchel is Gone

Eloy awoke next morning with a strange feeling inside. He glanced across to where Ixchel slept but her blanket was undisturbed. She had not come back. He wandered outside to look for her. No sign. Hadwin and Abha, also up and about, called the twins for breakfast; but only Eloy came.

'Where is your sister?' asked Hadwin.

'I don't know. I haven't seen her this morning.'

'Wandered off I expect,' said Hadwin. 'I told you, Abha, not to indulge her. Now I will have to go and find her.'

Abha served up the maize porridge she had been stirring, 'Leave her be, husband. Today is her birthday. I think we can forgive her one last day in the rainforest.'

'You are too soft on her,' said Hadwin, banging his spoon on the table. 'Very well, she may have today but tomorrow you keep her close. I don't want to be hunting her on the morning of the betrothal ceremony.' He guzzled down his porridge. 'Come on Eloy. Some of us have a long day in the fields ahead of us.'

Eloy gobbled down the remains of his porridge and followed Hadwin outside, casting his eyes at the rainforest for any sign of Ixchel; something wasn't right.

All day his thoughts were fixed on her. Usually, he could pick up on her mood or sense her presence even if she was away with Abha in the furthest fields; but today, nothing. By evening when there was still no sign of her, Hadwin was pacing outside their hut. Abha brought food out to him.

'I warned you woman. I warned you not to indulge her. If she doesn't return tonight, we will have to send out a search party and how will that make us look?' he said snatching the bowl off her. 'The village already laugh at us because of her wayward behaviour.' He glared at Abha. 'Don't think that I don't hear the gossip. As it is we have had to betroth her to someone from another village because no-one here will have her.' He hurled the bowl of food. 'You should have left her to die at birth. It would have been less trouble.'

Abha retreated inside. Eloy, who had heard the shouts went to comfort her, but she pushed him away. Outside, Hadwin still raged. Eloy knew better than to approach him when he was in this mood, so he crept away to his and Ixchel's corner of the hut, pulling back her blanket and wrapping it around himself to breathe in her scent. 'Where are you?' he whispered. He hunted through her few possessions looking for a clue. Spying a small woven mat in the corner, he lifted it and found her basket of treasures; a piece of bone; a porcupine quill, a small quetzal feather and curled at the bottom, the shed skin of a kingsnake. *These are precious,* he thought, *she wouldn't leave these behind if she were planning to run away. She will be back.* Comforted by this thought, he lay down to sleep, worn out from a long day's labour and worrying about his twin. Sleep came quickly but it wasn't restful. His dreams were wild; filled with vicious hunters chasing him through the rainforest. Every time he hid, they found him, sniffing out his hiding place, making him run again until he collapsed, exhausted, under a chechen tree. Jaguars patrolled around him. He lay with his hands in front of his face, awaiting the attack. It never came. Instead, a dark voice filled his mind.

'Come outside boy.'

He recognised the voice. 'Yes, Ek Balem.'

He rose from his bed and crept outside. The shadowy form of a large cat appeared at his side.

'Your sister has gone. She is safe with us and will not return to you. Do not look for her. Tell your parents however hard they search; they will not find her so do not try.'

'Where? Where has she gone? She wouldn't leave without saying goodbye to me.'

'She is gone from you, but she is happy and that is all I can tell you. Rest now, boy. Do not forget my message.'

'They won't believe me,' called Eloy. 'Please, come back,' but the shadow was gone. He crept back inside. *Why would you leave me without saying goodbye, Ixchel? Why? I know you didn't want to get married but we would still have had each other.* A hard knot formed in his stomach. He clutched her possessions to his chest, curled up into a ball and wept.

In the morning he woke with a muzzy head, struggling to shake off the heavy cloak of sleep. Gradually the memory came back to him; Ek Balem and the message about Ixchel.

His parents were talking together.

'Your sister has not come home,' said Abha, 'we will have to start a search.'

Eloy looked from one to the other, 'She is not coming home,' he said.

'Not until I drag her back,' said Hadwin.

'No, father. She is never coming home.' He relayed the message from Ek Balem.

Hadwin and Abha listened in disbelief. Could it be true? And if it was the will of a god, should they go against it?

'We still have to look for her. You must have been dreaming. Why would Ek Balem talk with you. We must consult the village priest,' said Hadwin. 'Now, boy,' he said seizing Eloy's hand and dragging him off.

At the village altar the priest was busy preparing the day's offerings. He smiled at them, his expression changing to a frown at the look on Hadwin's face. He pushed Eloy forward.

'Tell the priest about your message.'

Eloy recounted his message a second time. The priest listened carefully.

'There have been times when the gods communicate directly but it is usually part of a bloodletting ceremony. Did you really see a black jaguar, boy?'

'Yes,' said Eloy. 'I'm not lying.'

'Sighting a black jaguar can be a sign of catastrophe,' said the priest.

'Losing a daughter is a catastrophe,' snapped Hadwin.

'Yes, yes,' said the priest. 'I will perform a ritual to verify the boy's story.' He gathered up some herbs, took them to the altar, burnt them, breathing in the smoke. He then carried the pot to Eloy and wafted the smoke around him before taking a knife to make a small incision in Eloy's palm, adding a few drops of his blood to the pot of embers. After mixing in the blood, he added water and drank from the pot, closing his eyes and waiting. Eloy and Hadwin watched the priest's body begin to twitch and convulse as the potion did its work. When the spasms had passed, the priest opened his eyes and spoke to Hadwin.

'The boy speaks the truth. Your daughter has gone. Ek Balem's will is that you let her go.'

'Are you sure?' asked Hadwin.

'It is his will. You must obey,' said the priest.

Hadwin looked dumbfounded, 'Then I will accept it,' he said grudgingly. 'I must tell my wife.'

Eloy could sense his father's anger at this turn of events and walked a few paces behind him. When they got back, he waited outside while Hadwin broke the news to Abha, listening to her cries of anguish. When they came out, Abha's face was tear-stained and she seemed to have shrunk with grief.

'Go to the fields Eloy. We must go and tell Kan's family that there will be no wedding,' said Hadwin.

Eloy wandered off, sad and alone. 'Where are you, Ixchel?' he called. 'How could you leave?'

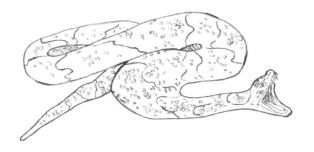

Chapter Seventeen

Snakebite

The months passed; Eloy worked the fields with
Hadwin as usual. Abha got used to the gossip
about her missing daughter, setting to her own
work and shutting out the pain of losing a child,
but she was diminished. Every day she woke and
left an offering at the village altar for her
daughter's return. Sometimes she left flowers,
other times food; always hoping that Ixchel would
come back to them, despite what the priest had
said.

Kan's family had been angry and demanded the return of the dowry items and more besides, but when a new bride was found for him, they quickly forgot about Ixchel.

Eloy grew taller and more muscular that summer. Hadwin looked at his boy and dreaded the visits from King Cadmael's men looking for recruits to the army. The conquests may have ceased but it took a large number of soldiers to maintain order in the other cities and to keep the tributes pouring into the king's coffers. Every few months, more young men were taken to join the ranks of the army. *Eloy's young and strong, he's bound to be chosen,* thought Hadwin sadly, *and then I will lose another child.*

The physical work sat well with Eloy, distracting him from constantly thinking about Ixchel. Dawn saw him rise and leave the house and wander into the forest, searching for any sign that she had been near. However hard he looked though, there was nothing.

Eloy wore the snakeskin she had treasured around his neck, a talisman and keepsake of his lost twin. One morning as he sat on a low branch of a zapote tree, staring up at the sky and wondering where she was, a kingsnake sidled up next to him. Eloy kept perfectly still, watching the

167

snake carefully. The two locked eyes. Eloy knew that he was being assessed; for what though? When the snake noticed it's discarded skin around Eloy's neck it sank its fangs into his arm. He yelled in pain and surprise but didn't move as the snake latched on.

'Why do you wear my skin? Do you think of it as a trophy to represent my brothers that your people have killed?' it said.

Shocked, Eloy realised that he had understood the snake.

'It was my sisters. I wear it in her honour. She is…she has gone from us.'

The kingsnake released his hold. Behind the boy he could see the shadow of a jaguar and he recoiled. 'I am sorry,' he said. 'Forgive my ignorance. The venom's effects will wear off by midday tomorrow. I have not given you a lethal dose.'

The wound on his arm bled and he felt the throb of the venom coursing through his veins. He scratched and scratched at his skin trying to stop the burning sensation and slow its progress, his eyes pleading with kingsnake for help. The venom hit his heart like a lightning bolt, paralysing him.

The snake disappeared, leaving Eloy alone and helpless on the branch of the tree.

What did he mean, his ignorance? thought Eloy, amidst the panic pressing in on him. A second wave of pain crashed through him and he passed out.

The morning was well advanced before Hadwin found him. He came looking when Eloy didn't appear either at breakfast or in the fields. His first thought, when he saw him lying on the branch was that he was sleeping.

'Get down here, Eloy, there is work to do. You cannot spend the day sleeping in a tree.' He waited.

'I said get down here.'

Incensed, he reached up to him, all anger falling away when he saw the fang marks.

'I'm sorry, my boy.' He scooped him up gently. 'I will be careful. I know the venom is painful.'

Once down from the tree he rushed home and sent Abha for the healer and the priest. They came with an herbal elixir that was gently poured down Eloy's throat and a poultice for the wound to try and draw out some of the poison.

'We must pray to the gods Ahau-Chamahez and Cit-Bolon-Tum,' said the priest. 'They are the only ones that can help him now.'

Eloy regained consciousness, listening to his parent's anxious voices, but unable to move, he could do or say nothing to reassure them that he would survive.

'Always our boy,' cried Abha. 'If the king's hunt were not enough, now a kingsnake attacks him. Haven't I suffered enough with the loss of my daughter. Now my son.'

'He is strong,' said Hadwin, hiding his own distress and trying to calm her. 'He will beat this. Come wife, let's go to the priest and make offerings.' He took her hand. 'Light some copal incense before we leave and when we return, we will keep vigil at his bedside.'

Eloy passed a painful night. His whole body felt like it was wrapped in needles. Dawn brought him some relief; the sting of the venom subsided. Now he had to wait for the paralysis to wear off. The first movement he had was his eyelids. Very slowly he blinked once. Abha, sitting patiently at his side, saw the movement and sprang up.

'Hadwin, husband, he is alive. He's alive. He moved.'

Unsure if he believed her, but wanting desperately for it to be true, Hadwin leaned over his son to see. Nothing. No movement.

'Woman you are too tired. There is no response. Look.' He picked up Eloy's limp and lifeless wrist that dropped back onto the blanket.

'He blinked,' said Abha, adamant that her son had moved.

They sat holding hands, watching, waiting, until finally, their patience was rewarded when Eloy managed to blink a second time.

'Thank the gods,' said Hadwin. He went outside picked the largest agouti from the pen and rushed to the priest to make an offering of thanks.

'My son lives. He lives,' he shouted.

The priest took the agouti and performed the sacrificial ritual, sending up prayers and thanks for the boy's life.

After his eyes, Eloy found movement gradually returning to his limbs. Just as the snake had said, the venom wore off by midday, enabling him to sit up and eat something.

To everyone in the village's amazement, the only outward after effect of the snakebite was a little stiffness for a few days. Eloy though, noticed that his hearing and sense of smell were greatly enhanced. He also found that when he sat with the men at village meetings to discuss various disputes that arose from time to time, he was able to see both sides of the argument clearly and could offer sound advice. He gained a reputation for suggesting fair and measured solutions. Often, men would approach him ahead of the meetings to seek his opinion. One evening the priest took him to one side and said, 'Eloy, I believe that you have been given the wisdom of the serpent. That is a mighty blessing. You have been greatly honoured.'

Eloy thought about this. 'I have felt differently since the kingsnake bit me. As if something were left behind when the venom passed.'

The priest pressed his hand on Eloy's forehead, breathing in deeply as he did so.

'I feel it too,' he said. 'You carry the mark of the snake. You will be a wise elder one day and a great protector of your village.'

'Me?' said Eloy, wondering if this was the destiny Ek Balem had meant.

'Yes, boy. The serpent represents wisdom. And there is something else, but it is clouded from me.'

'I wish Ixchel was here,' Eloy said. 'Why did she have to leave?'

'The gods have their reasons, Eloy. It is not for us to question them.'

'I know, Ah Kin, but I miss her so badly and my mother suffers terribly from her absence.'

'Loss is part of life, my boy. Use your inner wisdom to guide you forward. You have been blessed. Take comfort in that.'

Eloy wandered into the forest mulling over the priest's words.

'Ixchel,' he called. 'Ixchel, where are you?' but as usual there was no reply.

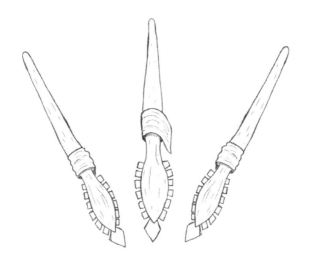

Chapter Eighteen

Conscripts

King Cadmael paced his throne room, trying to avoid the accusatory gaze of the statues carved into the back wall. Even the stone serpents' teeth that edged his throne looked ominous today. He had made three offerings that day; warrior slaves that should have pleased the gods, and yet his captains were still reporting unrest in the conquered cities.

'How dare they rebel against my rule and my taxes,' he railed at his High Priest. 'They should be honoured; honoured to have me as their king.'

The High Priest looked on nervously.

'Are you completing the rituals properly?' said King Cadmael.

'Yes, Ahaw.'

'Then why are the gods displeased!' he yelled, hurling his goblet of hot chocolate at the wall where it smashed into a thousand pieces showering the priest in the hot sticky liquid.

'Perhaps there are not enough soldiers,' ventured the High Priest.

'Not enough! Not enough! Then recruit more. Captain Bembe!' he bellowed.

Quick, heavy footsteps answered his call. The door to the chamber was opened by a thick-set man, arms and legs marked by scars, a sign of his years of battle experience. He knelt before the king.

'You summoned me, Ahaw.'

'You must recruit more men.'

'But Mighty Ahaw, we have recruited all those of fighting age.'

'Then take the younger ones and train them. Order must be maintained.'

The captain looked to the High Priest to assist him, but he said nothing.

'If that is your wish oh Great One, but…but the farmers may not like it.'

'The farmers. What do I care what the farmers like or do not like?' King Cadmael's face had turned a violent shade of puce. 'Follow my orders Captain or I will find someone who will.'

'Yes, Ahaw,' said Captain Bembe, rising and backing out of the room, cursing the luck that had made his family holders of the hereditary position of captain. Not for the first time he wished he had the luxury of relinquishing the title after three years like his counterpart, Captain Jacinto, to whom he passed on the king's orders.

'How dare he question my orders,' fumed King Cadmael. 'What have the farmers got to do with my conquests?'

'I think, Ahaw,' said the High Priest, nervously, 'that he meant the farmers need their sons to help with the growing and harvesting of the crops.'

'Let the women and girls do more. I must maintain order and, more importantly, I must please the gods.' He cast a glance at the statues behind him. 'Find out why they are displeased.' He waved him away. 'Go. Leave. Now.'

The High Priest scuttled away.

Having received his orders, Captain Jacinto sent men to all quarters of the city to take conscripts. Boys as young as eleven were rounded up and marched to the barracks, despite the pleas of their parents that they were too young. When they finished in the city, they moved outside to the farming settlements. Here they were met with open hostility. The constant drain on food stocks and their strong young men had made them angry. When the soldiers arrived at Hadwin's village, they were met by a wall of men and women brandishing spears.

'Do you wish to bring the king's fury down on you?' said the soldier in charge. 'He must have more men.'

'There are no more young men, only boys,' said Hadwin. 'Who will grow the food to feed his armies if you take them too? We need our boys.'

'So does the king,' replied the soldier. 'Now stand aside.' At a signal, his men advanced, quickly disarming the villagers. Each house was searched for the young boys that the villagers had tried to hide. Abha wanted to send Eloy to the cenote for water.

'Go, my boy, and wait there until the soldiers have left.'

'I am not a coward that I must hide, mother.' he said.

'I know, but the king thinks that you are dead. He is not a man to be crossed.'

'The king is not likely to see me and besides, that was many months ago, mother. I have grown taller since then and I have my beard coming,' he said, stroking his chin. 'No-one will remember me.'

Abha's eyes filled with tears, 'I don't want you to go,' she said. 'I have lost one child, I couldn't bear to lose another.'

'But mother, if they take the other boys and I am left, how will the village react? They will hate you and shun me. I must go with them.' He stood tall and resolute, looked straight at her and said, 'I promise you I will be safe.'

'You cannot make that promise,' said Abha, grabbing him and holding him tightly to her, whispering, 'Take care my son. May Ek Balem protect you.'

She released him and turned away. He left the hut without looking back and joined the rest of the boys that had been rounded up. *How young and frightened they all look,* he thought. The youngest one was Dacey, white with fear. Eloy knew that he had only seen ten summers so he went and stood next to him. Dacey glanced up at Eloy, who smiled and said, 'Be strong. Stay by me. I will take care of you.'

Chapter Nineteen

Training

The new conscripts were assembled at the army training grounds, a vast walled courtyard in a corner of the city. There was little or no shade and the heat bounced off the pale coloured stone driving up the already high temperature of the day. They were divided into groups of twenty before being assigned a trainer. The first thing to learn was how to use a shield effectively. When they had all been allocated one and lined up holding their shields in front of them, their trainer charged, spear in hand, at the first boy in the line. Eloy and the other boys recoiled at his screams when he failed to get his shield down in time and his leg was gored.

'Take him to the healers,' yelled Horado, their trainer, to a nearby soldier. He turned to the line of trembling recruits.

'This is what happens if you don't use your shield. You must be ready. Your enemy will show no mercy.'

He ran at the second boy, who just managed to parry the spear.

'Better,' said Horado.

Again and again, he ran at the boys who all managed to get their shields in the way in time. Then it was Eloy's turn. Although not trained in using a shield, his reflexes were quick and he was strong and muscular. Horado charged. Eloy parried the blow with strength and conviction, earning him a nod of approval. Last to face the trial was the diminutive Dacey who was shaking so much he could hardly hold his shield. 'You can do this,' Eloy whispered to him. 'Be brave, I am here.'

But as Horado rushed forwards, fear grabbed Dacey and he bolted into a corner.

'Come back, coward.'

Dacey crouched in a corner of the courtyard, sobbing. Eloy ran after him.

'Leave him!' ordered Horado, advancing quickly, eyes blazing, spear pointed. Eloy placed himself in front of Dacey, feet firmly planted, taking the full force of Horado's spear on his shield. His strong stance gave powerful resistance to the blow, knocking Horado off balance. The line of boys watched, unsure how to react.

Horado pulled himself up to full height and pressed his forehead to Eloy's.

'He is a child,' said Eloy.

'Child or not, he is mine now,' spat Horado, 'and he must train or die. Do you hear me boy?' He stared at Dacey who was too terrified to reply.

'Did you hear me?'

Dacey managed to nod. 'Get back in line.'

Eloy moved to go with him.

'Not you,' said Horado, placing a firm hand on his shoulder, then gesturing to a guard. 'Take him and give him ten lashes.'

Eloy was led away, watched anxiously by Dacey and the other boys.

'Time to get back to it,' said Horado, 'unless anyone else has anything to say.'

The boys all shook their heads.

He paired them up, giving one partner a stick and telling them to charge at the other. All except Dacey who he made run around the perimeter of the compound until he collapsed exhausted. Eloy found him there, after dark, bending down to gently shake him awake then taking his hand to help him to his feet. Dacey was too worn out and scared to notice Eloy wince in pain or see the blood trickling down his legs from the weals on his back that had broken open again. They made their way slowly to the sleeping quarters where Eloy shared his meagre food and water ration. Dacey began to cry again when he saw the damage on Eloy's back.

'This is m…m…my fault,' he sobbed.

'No,' said Eloy. 'It is the king's fault for making children fight his wars.' Eloy knew that it was dangerous to speak against the king, but he had experienced his callous cruelty.

'Sleep Dacey, you must be strong.'

'I…I'll try,' he said, although inside, he didn't know how.

The conscripts were roughly awoken at dawn by a kick from Horado. A breakfast of atole was followed by a long day on the training ground practising their shield work. Even with a stiff and sore back, Eloy was able to block all Horado's attacks, only adding to the older man's animosity towards him.

A training routine was established and over the course of several days the boys became much more competent with their shields. Even Dacey, with lots of encouragement from Eloy, gained in confidence and ability.

Next, was bow training. Eloy did not need any but when he tried to tell Horado this he was made to run the compound until told to stop. Each boy was measured against a bow. These were mostly weapons captured in previous raids. The matching took some time as the bow's length had to be just a little less than the height of its owner. Dacey's size proved to be a problem. All were too big, so one had to be cut down and remade. Once all the best bows had been allocated, Horado beckoned to Eloy to come and choose his. The remaining bows were cracked, scratched, old and bloodstained, but Eloy knew bows and found one that although shabby, still felt supple and strong.

Before any arrows were given out, the boys were taught how to handle the bow, how to stand when firing, and how to feel the tension in the bowstring to select the correct release point. Eloy knew what he was doing so he focused on helping Dacey until Horado noticed and interfered.

'You again. Why aren't you doing your own drills?' yelled Horado.

'Because I know how to use a bow,' replied Eloy calmly.

'You're only a farmer's boy. You know nothing,' scoffed Horado.

'Give me an arrow and I'll show you.'

Horado glared at him, then marched over to a pile of arrows and plucked three; he hung a shield on the far outer wall of the compound, over a hundred paces away. Eloy watched him, smiling to himself. This was going to be easy.

'Hit that,' said Horado, passing over the arrows.

'I only need one,' said Eloy, fitting the arrow and drawing back the bowstring.

'If you miss, it will be more lashes,' said Horado.

There was a collective holding of breath from the boys as they watched Eloy's arrow fly across the compound, followed by an uproarious cheer when

185

it hit the target, knocking the shield to the ground. Eloy lowered the bow and allowed himself the briefest smile when he saw the expression on Horado's face. The slap stung like a knife and sent him reeling backwards as the bow was wrenched from his hands.

'Problem with your recruits, Horado?' said Captain Jacinto, who had witnessed the assault.

'No Sir. Training Sir.'

The captain inspected the line of boys, squeezing their arms to check for muscles. He stopped in front of Dacey.

'How young are the children we are taking now?'

Dacey pulled himself up as tall as he could, but it couldn't hide his youth. Captain Jacinto sighed and then stared at Eloy.

'Why do you look familiar?'

Eloy, who recognised the captain from the hunt shook his head.

'Can he shoot that?' he asked Horado, pointing to the bow in his hand.

'Yes,' shouted one of the boys, wanting the captain to be impressed.

'Show me,' said Captain Jacinto, handing the bow to Eloy, who pretended to fumble and look incompetent. Horado, still furious, gripped Eloy's shoulders, shaking him violently, 'Show the Captain what you can do.'

Eloy looked at the eager faces of the boys, especially Dacey, who was so proud of his friend. A boy had been dispatched to rehang the shield. Taking an arrow, Eloy placed it in the bow and fired; once again, knocking the shield to the floor.

Realisation dawned on the captain. 'You are the boy from the hunt. We left you at the pit. The king must hear of this,' he said, grabbing Eloy's arm. 'Come with me now,' and he marched him straight to the throne room.

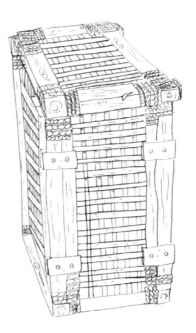

Chapter Twenty

Bad Omen

King Cadmael was not in the best of moods. Captain Bembe had sent reports of another uprising in the neighbouring city of Tikal that had been under his control for over a year.

'Why is this happening!' he screamed to his High Priest. 'I have the best soldiers. I ask only for fair tributes from these people.'

The High Priest raised his hands in a gesture that indicated he had no idea.

'This cannot be allowed. Send word to Captain Bembe that all protestors are to be rounded up and punished.'

'All of them, Majesty?' said the High Priest.

'Yes. I will not have my rule threatened. Send word now.'

The High Priest opened the throne room door, nearly colliding with Captain Jacinto, who stood there with his arm raised to knock. He regarded the young man behind the captain; there was something familiar about him. Instead of leaving he remained, curiosity getting the better of him.

'Ahaw,'

'Captain Jacinto. Why are you here? I thought you were getting me new recruits.'

'I was Majesty. I am. But then I encountered this one amongst them,' he said, shoving Eloy forward to the centre of the room.

'And why is he of interest to me?'

'Ahaw, look closely. This is the boy hunter. The one we left for the jaguars.'

King Cadmael strode towards Eloy, studying him carefully.

'You,' he said. 'You were left for jaguar fodder. For Ek Balem.' His face cleared.

'This is why the gods are angry and why the people rebel. You have displeased the gods not me.'

Eloy glared at the king, reliving the deep humiliation of their last meeting and the cruelty of the man. Somehow, he found his voice.

'The people rise up because they tire of your rule.'

'How dare you address me,' roared King Cadmael, striking Eloy across the face. 'No-one gave you permission.'

Still reeling from the blow, Eloy's face showed his defiance.

'Who helped you? You could not have survived on your own.'

Eloy remained silent. The king towered over him; hand raised to strike again.

'Tell me who helped you.'

'Ek Balem,' said Eloy, feeling the strength of the jaguar in his bones.

'Don't mock me boy. You are nothing but a farmer's son. Why would the jaguar lord help you?'

'Because I am not a monster like you.'

Incensed, King Cadmael struck him again.

'Captain Jacinto, go to the boy's settlement and round up all of them. They will pay for this insult.'

'No!' cried Eloy. 'They are not at fault.'

King Cadmael looked disdainfully at him, 'And Captain, take this insect away and lock him up.'

'Yes Ahaw.'

Eloy felt a rough hand on his arm, then he was marched to an area of the barracks that housed wooden cages used as holding cells for those awaiting execution.

'You may have escaped death once,' said the captain, shoving him inside a cage and tying it shut, 'but you won't this time.'

'Wait. Please,' said Eloy.

The captain stopped, turning back to face him.

'What will he do to my village?'

Captain Jacinto hesitated, then said, 'Most likely the king will sacrifice them all.'

'No, no.'

The captain shrugged, 'The king believes you are a bad omen and therefore so is your village.'

Captain Jacinto left to lead his soldiers to Eloy's settlement. He remembered where the boy had come from and how proud his father had been at his son's bowmanship. He thought of his own family that he hadn't seen for the two and a half years of his time as captain. Half a year more and his service would be completed, and he could return home. It couldn't come soon enough. He too had grown weary of the king's brutality and insatiable desire to increase his power at any cost.

Eloy grasped the bars of the cage shaking and shaking them, but he couldn't break free. *What was he to do? How could he save his village?* The merciless sun beat down on him. The cage was in the open and afforded him no protection from the heat. He had had nothing to eat or drink since breakfast; he was parched. His thoughts drifted to the forest and Ixchel. *I could do with your help again, sister.* But Ixchel was long gone.

Watching the heat haze rising up off the floor of the compound made him feel lightheaded. The next thing he knew he was being shaken.

'Eloy, Eloy,' whispered a boy's voice. 'Eloy, wake up.'

He stirred, raising an eyelid to see an anxious Dacey, peering through the bars.

'What are you doing here?' said Eloy, pulling himself upright. 'They will punish you if they catch you.'

'I brought you some water and cornbread,' said Dacey shoving a cup and a hunk of bread through the bars.'

Eloy downed the water in one long gulp before tearing ravenously into the bread.

'Thank you,' he said, grabbing the young boy's arm. 'Please go back and be careful.'

Dacey retrieved the cup and scuttled away before the guards came to check on the prisoner. A commotion broke out and his first thought was that Dacey had been caught. Fortified by the food and water, Eloy hauled himself to his feet to see what was going on. A troop of soldiers was shepherding a large crowd of people into the compound. He recognised his villagers, watching the people jostle with one another as they were being herded into the space, faces contorted with fear and confusion. Young children clung to their parents, babes-in-arms cried in distress. Then he picked out Hadwin and called to him. It took several shouts for Hadwin to hear him. He pushed his way through the throng of villagers, following his son's voice until he saw the cage and rushed over.

'Eloy, what's happening? Why are you in there? Why are we here?' he clutched his son's hands.

'The king blames me for the uprisings. He thinks that I am a bad omen because I survived the hunt.'

'Why the villagers? Everyone was rounded up.' said Hadwin. 'Soldiers came, forced us from our homes and fields, made us gather in the village centre and then brought us here.'

Eloy looked out at all the familiar faces; the village priest, Dacey's parents, the farmers he worked alongside, and their wives. 'What have I done? What have I brought upon you all?' he said, sinking to his haunches and weeping.

Hadwin knelt with him.

'Collective punishment,' whispered Eloy, through his sobs. 'I'm so sorry, father. You should have let me die at the pit.'

Hadwin put his hand on Eloy's chin, raising his head to look into his eyes.

'How could I do that? You are my son, and I would have done anything to save you.'

'Even if you'd known that this would be the outcome?'

'Even then,' said Hadwin, standing stiffly. 'I will go and find your mother and bring her here.'

A miserable Eloy watched him disappear into the throng.

Chapter Twenty-One
Eloy's Appeal

It was dark by the time Hadwin and Abha returned. Finding her had been difficult with so many people crammed into the compound. The three of them sat huddled together, holding hands through the bars, saying little, simply taking comfort in each other's presence, until, one by one they fell asleep. Eloy was the last one awake. The moon hung silently overhead, casting its watchful eye over the villagers. When its light glistened on his mother's face, he noticed how deep the lines around her eyes were and how, even in sleep, her face carried an embedded sadness. *Ixchel,* he thought. *How she misses you. We all do.*

The moon drifted on her way shrouding them in darkness. With her departure, Eloy finally slept. Jaguars filled his dreams. Everywhere he turned they appeared, surrounding him, and then, striding majestically through the centre of them, he saw a black jaguar. It walked right up to him. He reached out, placing a hand on its back. The other jaguars disappeared. He picked up the black jaguar and presented it to the king. The remainder of the dream passed in a haze of half-remembered scenes, jungle, jaguars, Ixchel.

He woke, to feel his cage being hoisted into the air by four guards. He was carried through the villagers in the compound for all to see his humiliation. More guards came and marched the villagers in a long procession behind the cage to the base of the pyramid. The King stood at the top. The High Priest waited lower down; he addressed them.

'Villagers, today you are honoured. King Cadmael has chosen you to be sacrificed to the gods to ward off any bad omens,' he stared directly at Eloy as he said this.

'You will ensure the continued success of the King's campaigns.'

The villagers looked at each other aghast. Even though it was regarded by some to be the ultimate honour to be sacrificed to the gods, to take a whole village when they had not been defeated by an enemy, was unheard of. The village priest bravely stepped forward, bowing low.

'Oh, great ones, may I ask why our village has been chosen for this honour?'

The High Priest pointed to Eloy, held aloft in his cage.

'Because you allowed that boy to live when the king had marked him for death.'

Eloy felt all the eyes of the villagers on him.

'Now you must appease the gods for your disobedience.'

'Wait,' shouted Eloy. 'Tell Ahaw that I would speak with him.'

'And why would he listen?'

'Because I will offer him something he dearly wants in exchange for my people.'

The High Priest sneered at him, 'What could you possibly offer the king?'

'Take me to him and you will find out.'

The High Priest said nothing, and Eloy was unsure he would get his chance to speak. Then he nodded to the guards to put the cage down and release him. The villagers watched on as the boy and the High Priest ascended the steps of the pyramid to the throne where King Cadmael sat, an imposing figure in his huge headdress and draped in jaguar skins.

'Why have you brought that thing here?'

The High Priest bowed, 'The boy wishes to make a plea for his village.'

King Cadmael laughed heartily. 'A fine jest, High Priest.' His expression changed, dark fury flashing across his face.

'Your Majesty, if I bring you a black jaguar, will you release my people?'

King Cadmael regarded Eloy.

'A black jaguar. And how do you propose to do that, they ran away from you last time we hunted?'

'You have seen me hunt. You know my skills. I can do this. I know that a black jaguar roams the jungle. I have seen it.'

'The boy talks nonsense,' said the High Priest. 'There is no black jaguar in these parts. I will begin the sacrifices.' He dragged Eloy away from the throne.

'Stop,' said King Cadmael. 'Come here boy.'

Eloy stepped closer to the king.

'You have seen one?'

'Yes,' said Eloy truthfully. 'More than once.' He did not of course, say that the jaguar in question was Ek Balem, God of the Underworld.

'And you believe that you can trap it?'

'I do.'

'I want it alive so that I can kill it.'

'Then you will be the only ruler to wear the black skin. That is a mark of mighty power, which must surely please the gods and you will have all the cities that you have not yet conquered, cowering in their beds.'

Eloy hoped the flattery would appeal to the king's vanity.

King Cadmael pondered Eloy's offer, picturing himself draped in the most precious of all jaguar skins.

'By the gods, you have until sunset two days from now to capture and bring a black jaguar to me.' he said. 'If you manage it, your villagers may return home. He grabbed Eloy by the hair, pulling his head backwards. 'Fail, and they will all be sacrificed. You last of all so that you can watch them all die for your mistakes.'

Eloy agreed. Before the king let him go, he added, 'You, of course, will be sacrificed whatever happens.'

He turned and left the throne.

The High Priest shoved Eloy down the steps.

'Take this creature to the edge of the city,' he ordered a guard, 'and let him go. And send that rabble down there back to the compound.'

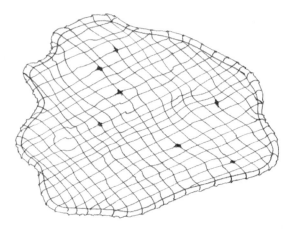

Chapter Twenty-Two

A Trap is Set

Eloy bolted home to gather his bow and arrows, a spear, rope and a net to set a trap. From inside, he scooped up some bread and fruits and a water container, putting them into a pouch he could sling over his shoulder. With a last look around he was about to leave when he remembered the snakeskin. Retrieving it from its hiding place, he wrapped it round his neck. 'Forgive me Ixchel,' he said, 'but I must save the village.'

He entered the rainforest, following the path he and Ixchel had taken to their meeting with Ek

Balem. He really had no idea how he was going to persuade a god to accompany him to the city, but he wouldn't allow any doubt to turn him from his mission.

The heat of the day felt heavy and oppressive and there was a smell of rain in the air. This was the season for sudden and violent downpours. He cast around for shelter. The only cover was the trees. He climbed up a ceiba tree as the first drops fell, creeping into a hollow between branches to sit out the storm. Looking up through the greenery of this, the tallest of trees, he could understand why his people regarded it as a symbol of creation. The branches appeared to reach the heavens, arms open, offering up blessings to the sky. The roots reached far down to the underworld, joining the earth and heaven.

'Blessed Ya'axche, sacred mother tree, thank you for keeping me safe,' he said. The tree did not reply but cradled him safely, lulling him to sleep. The light was beginning to fade when he woke. The storm, long since passed, had left behind puddles in the mud and released a fresh earthy scent from the plants, washed clean of dust and refreshed from their drink. Eloy, sat up and stretched, taking a drink from his own water skin. Sitting here scanning the horizon, he understood why Ixchel had felt so at home here. It was peaceful, no clashing weapons, no king, no priest; only nature, green and welcoming. Below him, a family of agouti emerged, snuffling about in the undergrowth for tasty morsels. Above him, a mockingbird whistled. He roused himself, his mission was urgent, and he had already tarried too long.

Climbing down from his perch, he went deeper into the forest until he reached the ring of chechen and chacah trees where he had me Ek Balem. Even in the fading light he could tell no cats had been there recently. The rain revealed no paw prints in the mud and there were no fresh droppings or discarded bones to indicate the presence of jaguar.

'No cats. They must have a new meeting place.' he said to himself. He decided to push on. It was a risk, jaguars hunt at night and he didn't want to find himself the prey again. Time was short and a lot of lives were at stake. He had no choice.

Quietly, cautiously, he picked his way, stopping every few paces to pick up leaves, checking for jaguar scent. Eventually, his patience was rewarded when he found fresh droppings and small animal bones. He hunkered down, listening; a faint splashing sound filtered through. Inching forward, the sound became clearer. A cenote, but who or what was swimming? He scouted around for the entrance, then decided it was too risky to go down it, not knowing what he would encounter. Instead, he skirted round and climbed up the mound that the pool sat underneath, hoping that there would be an opening for him to look through. He wasn't disappointed. Lying flat on his belly, he crawled forward and peered over the edge. There was definitely something swimming, he could hear the splashing and the tell-tale lapping of the water against the cave walls. It wasn't until the moon rose overhead and shone directly over the opening that he was able to make out what was in the water. Now he could see the long, slender shape of a big cat, swimming freely or diving down and resurfacing with a fish in its jaws. He was so intent on admiring the animal's graceful movements that it was some time before he realised that this cat lacked the usual mottled coat with its brown and black rosettes. It was in fact, the very thing he hunted; a rare and beautiful black jaguar.

Struggling to contain his excitement, he backed away from the opening.

'Thank you, Ek Balem,' he mouthed, 'thank you.'

He instinctively knew that it wasn't the jaguar god below him. This was a creature of the wild. Quickly and quietly, he scrabbled down from the roof of the cenote and retraced his steps to the entrance. He had to work fast; he had no idea how long the jaguar would remain in the water. Luckily, the cenote entrance was hidden by lush plants, that would camouflage his net. He spread it out on the ground a few paces from the entrance, covering it with loose leaves and bits of bark. His rope, he threaded through and around the outside to act as a drawstring, trapping the cat inside.

Trap set, he needed something to bait it, but what? He couldn't risk leaving to hunt down an agouti or turkey in case he missed it exiting the cenote. He realised there was only one thing he could use. Glad now, that he had drunk a lot earlier, he stood at the cave entrance and peed, leaving a trail in the direction of his trap. He sat just beyond the net where he would be in full view of the approaching jaguar and waited.

Dawn was approaching when the jaguar finally emerged from the cenote. It paused at the entrance, picking up the strange smell. Eloy watched its ears twitching, listening, before it stepped carefully forwards, following the scent, then stopped. Its keen eyes discerned the shape sitting a little way ahead. The morning breeze wafted Eloy's scent towards the cat. Instinct kicked in; this was an enemy. It crouched and sprang, landing a couple of paces in front of Eloy, teeth bared, growling menacingly. Eloy was on his feet the moment the jaguar landed, yanking on the rope, enclosing the enraged animal in his net before it had time to strike him. A great cacophony of hissing and hawing, like the sound of a saw on wood erupted from his captive. It was a female, he noted. The more the jaguar struggled, the more entangled it became. Eloy watched guiltily from a safe distance, praying that the noise would not bring other jaguars to investigate.

While the jaguar fought against her bonds, Eloy cut some large palm leaves and wove a makeshift pallet attached to two long branches he foraged from the surrounding trees. Next, he cut vines, plaiting them for strength, then tying them securely to the branches. When the jaguar finally lay still, utterly exhausted from her efforts to get free, he bravely bound its legs together with strong creepers preventing her from standing.

'I'm sorry girl, I have to do this,' he said. The net and its occupant he then hauled onto the pallet. Morning was well advanced by the time he had finished so he allowed himself the luxury of a nap in the shade to avoid the midday sun.

Refreshed from his short sleep, he took a dip in the cenote to wash off the sweat and grime of the last few days. Lying back in the water, his thoughts drifted away to lazy afternoons with Ixchel. He could hear her laughter echoing around the cave and picture the sheer joy on her face as she swam with total abandon. How he missed those childhood days. Now he had to take a beautiful jaguar that had been living free, to be slaughtered by a callous and vicious king, in order to save his village.

'Forgive me,' he called out.

Forgive me, forgive me, echoed off the walls, mocking his guilt. Heart heavy, he strode wearily out of the water to begin the journey back to Yaxchilan. The jaguar watched him, fear and anger etched on her face. She made several attempts to stand but the bindings held. Too ashamed to look the animal in the eye, Eloy lifted the plaited vines over his shoulders, heaving his burden along behind him.

Progress was slow. The afternoon hot and sticky, draining his energy. Sweat poured down his back attracting flies and other biting insects. The jungle felt denser somehow. Finding the cenote had been much easier. He often found his path blocked and impenetrable. The whistling of mockingbirds overhead grew louder, accompanied by rustlings in the undergrowth. If he didn't know better, he would have said that he was being followed. By evening he was exhausted, irritated, and ravenous. Observing the landscape around him, he was painfully aware of how little ground they had covered.

Too tired to go any further, he dug a hollow to light a small fire. Once it was well lit, he picked up his bow, left his precious cargo and crept stealthily to where he had spotted signs of agouti. He soon found one and dispatched it quickly, bringing the carcass back to feed himself and his prisoner. He skilfully skinned and butchered the agouti, wrapped his piece of meat in a leaf, placing it in the base of his fire, before tossing the rest to the jaguar. She sniffed suspiciously at the meat, then tore into it, eyes fixed on Eloy.

'I'm sorry,' he said, 'but I have to save my village and you are the price.'

He leaned against a tree to eat his meat. He didn't need to look up to know that the jaguar was still watching him. Warily, he moved closer to check on his prisoner. The cat remained motionless until her gaze alighted on the snakeskin around Eloy's neck. Something in her memory was awoken by it. Something lost yet important. She became more and more agitated, thrashing about trying to rip

209

her bonds. The more she fought the tighter they became, cutting into her flesh.

'Steady girl, steady,' said Eloy, desperately trying to work out what was causing this further distress. The jaguar's eyes were wild and she foamed at the mouth. Eloy had to back away for his own safety.

'What has spooked you?' he said, wiping sweat from his brow. His fingers brushed the snakeskin and realisation dawned. He removed it, holding it out to show that it wasn't alive. That only agitated the jaguar more as she struggled with her resurfacing memories. *What was the skin telling her?*

Eloy curled up the skin and placed it out of sight in his bag, not wanting to cause the creature any more distress. It seemed to help. She calmed down a little, but he could still see the tension in her limbs. He so badly wanted to let her go but he could not.

Sleep eventually found him, his body slumping to the floor. His dreams were full of black jaguars appearing everywhere he turned. Some were trussed up like his one, others rested in trees, yet more ran free. One sat side by side with him, resting a giant paw on his knee, only when he looked again, it wasn't a paw, it was a hand and beside him was Ixchel. He blinked, and now it was a black jaguar again. The rest of the black jaguars walked up to the one at his side and stepped into it until it became immense, towering over him like a jaguar-shaped pyramid. Then it was gone and Ixchel strode towards him. He reached out to grab her and wrap her into an embrace. She felt different, soft, furry and he wasn't holding Ixchel, he was hugging a black jaguar.

'Ixchel!' he screamed.

Chapter Twenty-Three

Reunited

He awoke, shaking, to find the jaguar staring at him. *Was that recognition on her face?* Tentatively, he crawled closer, unsure what drove him to her. Bravely he pressed his forehead to hers. She remained motionless.

'Ixchel? Ixchel is that you?'

In answer she licked his face and purred; deep within, she knew this was her twin. His arms were immediately wrapped around her neck so that he could press his face into her fur where it absorbed the tears pouring down. When his sobs subsided, he sat back to look at her.

'So, this is what became of you. You always climbed the trees like a cat, now I know why?'

She licked at her bonds.

'I can't,' said Eloy. 'Ixchel, I have made a bargain with the king. Your life in exchange for our entire village. Please, please forgive me. I can't free you.' As he spoke the words, he felt his heart tear in two.

Had she understood? He had no way of knowing. He waited, hoping for a sign that would show him what to do. Ixchel chewed at her bonds while guilt gnawed at his. The sun reflected off the emerald green of the jungle. Was it his imagination or had the trees moved closer, walling him in? He realised that there was no sound, no rustling, no bird song, even the breeze had ceased. It seemed like a million eyes were on him, although he could see none. The forest was waiting for his next move. Would he make the right one?

Pulling his short blade from his waist, he leant across and cut the vines from Ixchel's feet. The jungle exhaled. He felt the breeze sigh in relief and heard the resumption of the small animal noises on the ground and the birdsong above.

'Right choice,' a voice in his head said. He untangled his net from around Ixchel, rolling it back up and tying it neatly, watching as she got to

her feet and stretched luxuriously, arching her back and pushing her forelegs out straight in front of her. She licked his face and bounded away.

He watched her go then sat with his head in his hands. *What had he done? He had just condemned his village to death. How could he face them?* A kind of inertia, settled on him, a leaden cloak of listlessness. His brain tortured; if I stay here, they die; if I go back, they die. Unable to decide, his desolate mind paralysed him for the entire day. Anyone passing by might have thought that he was dead, sitting there with his eyes staring blankly straight ahead. Flies bit his skin and he didn't flinch. A few curious agoutis sniffed around his feet, but they too failed to get a reaction. His mind was paralysed with guilt.

It wasn't until nightfall that a change happened. A rough tongue licked his face, freeing him from his stupor. Ixchel sat beside him.

'You came back,' he said, grasping her tightly, not wanting this moment to end. When he finally let go she pressed her forehead to his and he felt her strength flowing through him.

'Ixchel, my dearest sister, what am I to do? I can't give you to the king but how else are we to save our parents and the villagers?'

Ixchel gave a low growl and gripped his tunic in her jaws, hauling him to his feet. She walked slowly away.

'You want me to follow you?' said Eloy.

Ixchel looked back at him then began sprinting through the jungle. Eloy followed as fast as he could, ripping through the undergrowth to keep up with his sister. Faster and faster they ran. He had no idea where they were heading but it didn't matter. The pure joy and freedom of running was exhilarating. The wind in his hair cooled him, the aromatic scents of passionflower and copal resin filled his nostrils.

'You said that you would outrun me one day,' he shouted.

As he ran, he sensed movement on either side of him but he couldn't make out what it was. The longer they ran, the greater the sensation. Something was definitely running with them. The terrain began to feel familiar as Ixchel slowed down and he was able to look around. They passed the deserted fields and entered their village, stopping at the altar.

Eloy bent over, panting heavily. When he straightened up, he found himself face-to-face with another jaguar, its familiar golden coat patterned with brown and black rosettes had perfectly camouflaged it.

'It was you that ran beside me!' said Eloy. At a growl from this jaguar another one appeared and then another and another. Line after line of jaguars emerged and gathered around the twins; more of the big cats than he could count. Their presence gave off an air of immense power and strength. Eloy, over-awed and terrified, clung tightly to Ixchel. He felt their combined gaze on him. They took their lead from Ixchel, as long as she was beside him he would be safe.

The jaguars roared in unison and sat up tall, forming a pathway down which strode Ek Balem. Eloy jumped to his feet to bow to this mighty god. Ixchel lay on her four paws, head down, showing her respect in cat fashion.

'My dear twins,' he said, 'I have brought you back to the place of your birth as the long-awaited day of your destiny is upon us.' He stopped in front of them. 'Eloy, your birth was anticipated by the gods and greatness awaits you. This much has always been known.' He surveyed the host of waiting jaguars, before continuing. 'What has always been hidden until recently, was why you came into this world with a twin.'

Eloy and Ixchel moved closer together.

'You now know, Eloy, that Ixchel is a child of the jungle. She has always belonged to me and I have claimed her. But before she can be truly free, you must fulfil your bargain with the king. This is why your sister was born.'

'No. How? I can't let him kill her.'

'You assume too much, boy. Have you not looked around you,' said Ek Balem. 'Do you think her family will let her go alone?' The jaguars roared their response. 'They know what to do. Everything is in place. Eloy, walk with me. This is the plan.'

Eloy listened to the plan, throwing up his hands in disbelief. 'How can I be the one to do this? I am only a village boy.'

'You have always been so much more,' said Ek Balem. 'Look into your heart. Your life here has never satisfied you because it was never where you were meant to be.'

Talking ended, Ek Balem roared thunderously, breathing renewed vigour and courage into Eloy's soul.

'Rise up and claim your place, my son.'

And then he was gone.

Chapter Twenty-Four

The Black Jaguar

Following Ek Balem's departure, Eloy and Ixchel set off for the city, the boy and the jaguar side by side. The other jaguars followed at a discreet distance. This time the forest parted easily, placing a path in front of them that led to the outer walls of the city. It was daybreak when they arrived, so they sought shelter amongst the trees and rested. It was the day Eloy was due back, but they could not enter the city until dusk, so they waited. If you had gone into the forest that day you would have seen one hundred jaguars gathered together and run away, terrified. If you were brave enough to linger, you might also have noticed the teenage boy that slept in their midst, his head resting on the paws of a majestic black jaguar, and marvelled at his audacity.

Inside the city, King Cadmael paced impatiently. Reports of insurrections were still coming in. His men were managing to quell them but it meant delays in his tributes which angered him. However, it was the constant attempts to defy his power and control that really made him furious. He cursed himself for making a bargain with the village boy; he should have just killed him there and then and removed the bad omen from his reign and campaigns. He summoned the High Priest.

'We must start the sacrifices immediately. Gather the offerings.'

'But the boy has until sunset,' said the High Priest.

'He has until I say he has.'

The High priest did not move.

'What? Why are you defying me?'

'Mighty Ahaw, my king,' said the High Priest. 'We must give the boy until dusk or the gods will be displeased because you broke your word.'

King Cadmael felt the veins in his temple throbbing at this latest challenge to his authority, but even in his anger he knew better than to cross the gods.

'Very well, but I want the offerings prepared. The sacrificial ceremony will begin at dusk, starting with the boy's father.'

The High Priest bowed and retreated from the room barking commands to the other priests: to set jars of copal incense in place ready to light at dusk; to sharpen their sacrificial knives; and put on the appropriate robes and body paint. He found Captain Jacinto to inform him how the evening would proceed.

Once again, the villagers found themselves being ushered to the pyramid. Captain Jacinto sought out Hadwin and Abha putting them at the front. The villagers were then divided into two rows; men and boys in one line, women, girls and babes-in-arms in the other. They were then marched up the pyramid steps in single file. At the top step, Hadwin and Abha were told to stand. In this way, as each sacrifice was completed, they could move up in an orderly fashion until it was their turn to meet the sacrificial knife. Captain Jacinto knew that as the ceremony went ahead a river of blood would flow down the steps. He looked at the frightened villagers in his charge and turned to his second in command, 'I have seen many battles and witnessed countless sacrifices of those we conquered, but this wanton bloodshed of babies and children, I have no desire to see.'

'The gods must be appeased though, Captain.'

'But surely there is another way. Would you want this for your family? I would not.'

'There is nothing we can do, my Captain.'

'Except pray for a miracle. Perhaps the boy will be successful.'

******

At the gloaming, Eloy, head held high, walked determinedly into the city, taking the central route towards the pyramid. Ixchel and the jaguars did not accompany him. They would make their way secretly through the narrow passages, ensuring they remained unseen. Most of the population had been corralled into the pok-a-tok court to witness the ceremonial sacrifices, so the jaguars' paths were largely unencumbered. If anyone had seen them, they would not have believed the boldness of such creatures to venture into the city.

Eloy passed the soldiers' compound where the new recruits, alerted by outrunners of his approach, had gathered on top of the wall to watch. Dacey bravely shouted out Eloy's name and was rewarded with a friendly wave. Eloy pushed his way through the crowds at the pok-a-tok court to the base of the pyramid. Pausing, he breathed deeply, knowing that the jaguars were close by, having seen the glinting eyes of Ixchel in the darkness.

King Cadmael emerged from his throne room wearing his mightiest headdress. No-one was going to question his authority tonight. He advanced to the centre of the pyramid to address the offerings.

'Villagers, you are here to offer yourselves in sacrifice to the gods. This is a great honour that has befallen you.' He paused to see the effect of his words.

'You are aware that your settlement was chosen because one of your own, the boy Eloy, was marked by me for death. However, his parents kept him alive. This has angered the gods. Tonight that displeasure will be rectified.'

The children's crying grew louder as they clung tightly to their parents.

'I did offer you mercy if the boy returned here tonight with a black jaguar. As you can see, he has failed.' He beckoned to his High Priest. 'You may begin the ceremony.'

With a glance in Ixchel's direction Eloy strode forward.

'King Cadmael,' he shouted, climbing the pyramid stairs. 'Do you not honour your promises?'

King Cadmael turned to look down the steps, the veins in his temple throbbing again.

'You told me that I would witness every sacrifice and yet you are about to start without me.'

Hadwin called to his son, 'No Eloy, no.' One of the other priests restrained him.

King Cadmael laughed, a cruel smile spreading across his face as Eloy approached him.

'Brave words. Very well, you may have your wish, seeing as you have failed to do what you promised.' He clicked his fingers and a priest grabbed Eloy, tying his hands and roughly standing him at the base of the altar. Abha reached out her arms to her son, tears glistening in the evening light. He smiled back at her.

The lower ranked priests, the Chilanes, pulled Hadwin forward, painted his chest and legs in a special blue paint and placed a cone shaped cap on his head. The round altar stone was anointed in the blue paint to cast out any evil spirits, then Hadwin was very swiftly laid on his back upon the altar.

King Cadmael watched on, relishing in the discomfort of Abha and the villagers.

'See what you have brought upon your family, boy, with your overconfident promises,' smirked the king.

Eloy glared directly at King Cadmael, 'It is you who are overconfident,' he said, whistling a long low note. Cadmael laughed.

'Is that supposed to scare me?'

'No', said Eloy. 'She is.'

Ixchel and her jaguars charged up the pyramid steps. The High Priest screamed, threw down his headdress and ran away as fast as he could. The other priests were cornered by several jaguars and stood cowering at their bared teeth. Ixchel chewed through Eloy's bonds and together the two of them converged on the king.

'Your black jaguar, Ahaw,' he said with a mock bow, 'and her friends.'

King Cadmael stared at Eloy standing there with his hand placed casually on the jaguar's back as if it were the most natural thing in the world.

'She is all yours.'

Ixchel took a step forward, eyes fixed on the king. She growled menacingly, echoed by the host of jaguars that lined up behind her. Momentarily frozen, he stared back, then throwing off his headdress he turned and ran pursued by Ixchel and the jaguars, his terrified screams ringing out across the night sky until they fell ominously silent.

Eloy picked up the King's discarded headdress and placed it in one of the braziers that lit up the pyramid.

He addressed the villagers and the crowd below who had witnessed the scene in stunned silence.

'Good people of Yaxchilan, the reign of King Cadmael is over. No longer will your children be sent to fight his wars.'

Hadwin and Abha rushed to embrace their son. The villagers cheered his bravery. Captain Jacinto rallied his men, all stunned by what they had witnessed, and marched up to Eloy.

'Have you come to arrest me, Captain?' he asked. 'If you have, my sister and her friends may take issue with you.'

Ixchel and the jaguars walked back up the pyramid and surrounded Eloy. Captain Jacinto noticed the bloodstains around the jaws of some of the cats and knew for certain that King

Cadmael's reign was done. Keeping a careful watch on the predators he knelt in front of Eloy.

'You have defeated King Cadmael,' he said. 'That makes you our new ruler, Ahaw, if you wish it, and I give you my loyal service.'

Ixchel circled her brother and sat up tall at his side. Eloy stroked her head, stood proudly and contemplated the offer.

'Thank you, Captain, I accept.'

Chapter Twenty-Five

Farewell

Watched on by the jaguars, Captain Jacinto and his men escorted the relieved villagers down the pyramid and then he sent an armed guard with them to the edge of the city. Hadwin and Abha bombarded Eloy with questions.

'How did you find a black jaguar?'

'How did you command the other jaguars?'

'What did you mean, Your sister?'

'What happens now?'

'Are you really the king now?'

'Enough.' laughed Eloy. 'I will explain everything. But first, say hello to Ixchel.'

Ixchel, purring loudly, looked up at her parents. Hadwin and Abha glanced at each other, mystified.

'This is what became of her,' said Eloy. 'Ek Balem claimed her as his own and transformed her.'

'How can you be sure?' asked Hadwin warily.

'Because father, I have spoken with him.'

'Then you are truly blessed my son,' said Hadwin, kneeling before him.

'Father, do not kneel. I am still your son.'

Abha had ceased listening; she was staring at Ixchel, who sat calmly beside Eloy. Very, very tentatively, Abha reached out to touch Ixchel's head.

'My girl,' she said. 'My girl.'

Ixchel purred, recognising her mother, who suddenly wrapped both her arms around the jaguar's neck and held on tightly. Ixchel responded by licking Abha's face.

'See, Hadwin, it really is our child.'

Cautiously, Hadwin stroked the jaguar's back, tears streaming down his face.

'I am not sure how long she will stay with us,' said Eloy. 'When she returns to the jungle she will have to stay away from humans. Even though I will never hunt jaguar, other rulers will, and she is the most prized of all.'

'Won't she miss us?' asked Abha.

'I think she will forget us. When I caught her, she didn't know who I was, nor I her. It was this snakeskin that triggered her memory,' said Eloy pointing to the one back around his neck.

Their reunion was interrupted by the return of Captain Jacinto who guided the family to the king's chambers where they could comfortably spend time together.

When they eventually retired to bed, Ixchel slept next to Eloy just as they had done before. For a time, the family were happily reunited.

In the ensuing days, Captain Jacinto and Captain Bembe guided Eloy through his royal duties, preparing him for his kingship and coronation. At every meeting Eloy was accompanied by Ixchel, his own personal bodyguard.

The royal scribes were kept very busy recording all the changes. Envoys were sent to the cities that King Cadmael had conquered to begin the transition back to self-rule and ensure the safe return of soldiers. A new High Priest had to be appointed too.

Three weeks after the defeat of King Cadmael, the day came for Eloy to be crowned. The new High Priest attended to his ruler, ensuring the royal robes were just perfect before presenting him with a magnificent wooden headdress, carved with the head of a serpent to show his wisdom and painted in the colours of the jaguar to represent his strength and courage.

'Majesty, Ahaw, you have no quetzal feathers. A king must have the feathers of the quetzal.'

'There is no need,' said Eloy.

'But sire, the birds are sacred.'

'Yes,' said Eloy. 'That is why there will be no need to take their feathers.'

The High Priest was perplexed by this. No previous ruler had ever had a headdress without the adornment of quetzal feathers, it was a symbol of truth and light. Seeing the puzzled look on his face, Eloy said,

'High Priest, my reign will bring many changes to our people. One of which is that we will no longer simply take from the animals because we like their skins or their feathers.'

'I don't understand. Why not?'

'Because we must treat them as we would our friends. The jungle is theirs as much as ours, perhaps more so.'

'That is a lofty ambition, Majesty.'

'I know, High Priest, but that doesn't mean it is unachievable.' He took a few moments to gather his thoughts then said, 'I am ready.'

The High Priest opened the door to the royal chamber and inhaled sharply. Ixchel waited outside with a quetzal bird on her back which flew up and alighted on top of Eloy's headdress. He smiled knowingly at the High Priest, who bowed respectfully.

Ixchel took her place at her brother's side, then the two of them strode forward through a phalanx of seated jaguars marking the way to the throne. When he reached the temple at the top of the pyramid he could see a jaguar sat on every step to honour his coronation.

At the base, the citizens waited to see their new ruler and hear him speak.

'People of Yaxchilan, today marks the dawn of a new era for our city. I am making peace with our neighbours and returning us to prosperity.' Cheers from the crowd.

'Some of you know me as Eloy, but from today as your king, I will be known as Shield Jaguar, in honour of the mighty Ek Balem, who has been my guide; and our city will be known as The Jaguar Kingdom.' He held out his arms to the people.

'Many changes are coming, but for now, go and celebrate this day. There is food and dancing to be enjoyed.'

And that is what the citizens of Yaxchilan did. The joyful celebrations went on for several days; everyone so pleased that the cruel and oppressive reign of King Cadmael was over.

A few nights after the ceremony, Eloy awoke to find Ixchel pacing his room, clearly agitated.

'What's wrong?' he said, climbing out of bed to go to her. Her fur bristled at his approach.

'It's time, isn't it? Time for you to go.'

He opened the door, and she ran through. Eloy went to the chamber where his parents slept and woke them up.

'What is it?' mumbled Hadwin sleepily.

'Ixchel is leaving,' he said. 'Come on.'

They got up and followed him. He had picked up her trail and knew which way she had gone. They found her sat on the throne staring out beyond the city. She growled at their approach, but then climbed down and came towards them, circling each of them before rubbing her forehead against them in a farewell gesture. Abha sobbed, bravely clutching Ixchel around the neck until the growls made her let go.

Hadwin too had tears in his eyes. 'Goodbye little one. We love you,' he said.

Then it was Eloy's turn. She placed her front paws on his shoulders and nuzzled his forehead while his arms wrapped around her, holding on tightly. The breeze began to swirl, she sniffed the air. The forest was calling. Eloy let go and she walked a few paces away. The family, hearts bursting, held hands, tears falling. With one last look back, Ixchel roared and bounded down the pyramid and away to her beloved forest.

'Do you think we will ever see her again?' said Abha, between sobs.

'No,' said Eloy. 'She has gone to where she belongs, but at least you now know what has become of her and that she is happy.'

There was a movement behind them, and they turned to see another, larger black jaguar sat on the throne.

'Ek Balem,' said Eloy, bowing low and indicating to his parents to do the same.

'You have done well, Eloy. Your sister has fulfilled her role, now you must fulfil yours. Greatness is not in the title of king. Greatness comes from the way you treat people and the land. I will be watching. You have the making of a wise and fair king. You have walked with jaguars just as the prophecy says. I wish you well.'

And then he was gone.

Abha and Hadwin stared, open-mouthed. Too shocked to speak. Eloy led them back to their room and the three of them sat together for a while discussing the night's events.

'You really have spoken with a god,' said Hadwin.

'Imagine humble farmers like us being in such a great presence,' said Abha.

'And how is it that our family was chosen for such honour?'

'It is not where you start in life that matters,' said Eloy, 'but how you use the opportunities you are given. I almost squandered my chance. I let pride take over me. Ixchel never did.'

The mention of her name, silenced them and they sat quietly thinking about the wayward girl who had become queen of the jaguars.

******

Eloy, Shield Jaguar, ruled well and brought great wealth to his city in his long sixty-year rule. Ek Balem watched on, but only visited him once more. Yaxchilan became one of the greatest of the Mayan city states and remained so for many years, ruled over by his descendants who each walked under a frieze of jaguars as they took the throne.

Epilogue

Five years into his reign, on the night of his birthday, the cusp between the months of Zip and Zotz, Eloy felt the call to the rainforest jungle. He rose from his bed, pulled on some moccasins and a dark tunic and crept from his chamber, taking care to avoid being seen by the guards. Calling on all his old hunting skills, he crept stealthily out of the royal dwelling and made his way out of the city. Although he hadn't walked the old path for years, instinctively he knew the way and soon found himself in the familiar grove of chechen and chakah trees. A black jaguar sat patiently waiting. The night was still and a full moon hung in the sky. A gentle rustling alerted the jaguar to an approaching figure.

'Eloy, welcome,' said Ek Balem.

Eloy bowed. 'You called me.'

'Yes, my son. The gods are very pleased with you. I am pleased with you.'

Eloy bowed a second time. 'Thank you mighty one. I am glad.'

'It is your birthday. I have brought a gift.'

'For me?'

Eloy felt someone entwine their fingers with his and a girl stood next to him.

'Ixchel, Ixchel. How?' he spluttered before embracing her tightly.

'Every five years,' said Ek Balem, 'on the anniversary of your births, for one hour either side of midnight, you can be reunited, here, as long as you tell no-one and are not discovered. This is my gift.'

And there the two of them sat, brother and sister reunited, holding hands under the stars, watched over by Ek Balem, God of the Underworld.

Author's Note

Whilst the Mayan city of Yaxchilan was known as The Jaguar Kingdom, and one of its rulers was known as Shield Jaguar, this version of how that came to be is entirely my own. I was inspired by the frieze of jaguars that the rulers had to walk beneath and I wanted to add my own interpretation to events. Mayan history is so rich, and we are only just beginning to understand the full extent of that wonderful civilisation.

Acknowledgements

My thanks as always go to my fellow StoryVine members, Sue Newgas, Jenny Heap and Rowen Wilde for their continued support and friendship. To my son Phillip for his honest feedback and moral support when I needed it and for accompanying me to visit the ruins of Ek Balem in Mexico and swimming in the cenote with me. To Kara too, who helped me find the courage to abseil down the guide rope into the water. What an experience!

Thank you once again to Leo Hartas for producing another brilliant cover for me. Thank you to Alan Sharpe for his splendid illustrations.

A massive thank you to my editor, Becky Stradwick, without whom this book would not have been anywhere near as good. Becky your insights really elevated this book and helped me to develop it into a much better story.

Thank you to my advance readers; Siddanth Seshadri, Arush Kothamatchu, Sreedaksh Bhupathi, and of course Phillip Daneshyar.

And finally, thank you to you for reading this book and posting a positive review on the site of your choice (if you have). I hope that you enjoyed this story and will tell all your friends.

To find out more about me and my books go to www.terridaneshyar.com where you can sign up for my newsletters or find me on Facebook, terri daneshyar author.

About the Author

Terri lives in Warwickshire with her husband, youngest son and two cats. Her love of stories began with her father who'd make up magical tales to delight his children. An avid reader, her attachment to works of fantasy was cemented by the likes of Tolkien and the Thousand Nights and One Night. As a child she was enchanted by the tales of Hans Christian Anderson, the Brothers Grimm and other folk tales from around the world.

Terri worked for many years as a primary school teacher where she hoped to instil her love of stories and reading to future generations. These days, when she's not working on her next book, she will either be reading someone else's, or watching cricket; her other big passion. No surprise then, that her lead character in The Light Stone series, is named after a cricket player!

Works published by Terri Daneshyar

The Treasure Thief

Stolen treasures

A missing professor

Mysteries unravelled.

When Lottie's father goes missing from his archaeology dig, she's left in the care of her stern Aunt Helen. This is not how Lottie had planned to spend her summer. But things take an unexpected and exciting turn when Aunt Helen decides that they will go to Lebanon, the last place her father was seen, to uncover the truth of his disappearance. Using clues left by her father, Lottie and her new friend Amir, decide to track him down, setting off a perilous chain of events: kidnap, a car crash and a race out to sea.

The adventure is available here: www.terridaneshyar.com

Betty's Bones

Eight-year-old Betty is a fossil finder and dinosaur hunter. When she tries to give her discoveries to the local museum, the Curator thinks she's just a nuisance and sends her away. But when she finds something really special and the Natural History Museum comes calling, things get more exciting than she could have ever imagined...

Visit: www.terridaneshyar.com

YA Fantasy

The Light Stone Series

Paladin

Something dark haunts the Shaman-Master's apprentice. Do the Paladin trust him or is betrayal inevitable? A were-spider, a were-snake and an intuitive bowman make up the Paladin, who serve as elite ambassadors for the Shaman-Master. His apprentice Jadeja, leads an ordered and safe life. When he is tasked with leading the Paladin on a hunt for three sacred power stones, the Shaman-Master's only hope to banish an all-powerful demoness, he feels certain to fail.

Protected by sacred runes, they embark on their quest. Dark voices haunt Jadeja and the Paladin don't trust him. They are pursued by a ruthless enemy as Jadeja guides them on an adventure where they battle terrible monsters and face their deepest fears. But what awaits Jadeja is far worse than he could ever contemplate...

Buy the book to experience this adventure today.

www.terridaneshyar.com

The Light Stone Series

Lamenter

Out of darkness

The light bearer comes.

Vikander is Paladin to the Shaman-Master, sworn to protect him and the Temple of Shang To. But he is betrayed by those closest to him at a time of great danger for the Temple, setting off a chain of catastrophic events. A hidden labradorite crystal opens a portal, allowing demons to attack the temple. The Light Stone, a talisman of immense power, is stolen, releasing a monstrous demoness, and an act of misguided bravery leads to disaster.

When Vikander is called upon to lead the quest to capture the demoness, he doubts that he will have the courage. He must ride the mythical, fire-breathing chimera and survive. Will he and his allies act in time to stop the demoness from making a terrible sacrifice that will tie her to the Light Stone forever?

Buy the book here www.terridaneshyar.com